VISIONARY ARCHITECTURE

Ernest Burden

VISIONARY ARCHITECTURE

UNBUILT WORKS OF THE IMAGINATION

McGraw-Hill New York San Francisco Washington, D.C.
Auckland Bogota Caracas Lisbon
London Madrid Mexico City Milan
Montreal New Delhi San Juan
Singapore Sydney Tokyo Toronto

Dedication

The work in this book was produced by architects, artists and designers who remained outside of the main-stream, whose work was ignored at the time, or who refused to make compromises. This book is dedicated to all those who have followed their imagination in the past, and to all those who will follow their imagination in the future, no matter where it will lead them.

The Library of Congress cataloged the First Issue as follows:
VISIONARY ARCHITECTURE:
Unbuilt Works of the Imagination. 1st-ed.

McGraw-Hill

A Division of The McGraw·Hill Companies

1 2 3 4 5 6 7 8 9 0 QKP/QKP 9 0 4 3 2 1 0 9

ISBN 0-07-008994-9

This book was designed and produced by Ernest Burden

Cover / Illustration: **Gilbert Gorski**, Demeter and Dionysus
Cover / Design: **3r1 Group**
Cover / Art Direction: **Margaret Webster-Shapiro**, McGraw-Hill, Inc.

Printed and bound by: Quebecor / Kingsport

Preceding Title Page:
The Fifth Element Still image from Columbia Picture's science fiction fantasy (Computer image by: Digital Domain#11 1998) (Courtesy of Photofest, New York City)

Preface

This collection of drawings by artists, designers, delineators and architects represents three distinct but overlapping categories of art and architecture each with its own styles, forms and concepts.

One of these embodies architectural visions; another embraces visions of architectural forms, and the third expresses design as visionary architecture. They are all concerned with the "art of building" but in totally different ways.

No distinction has been made in the presentation of the work between an architectural structure as a final buildable product, or as the study and expression of architectural form. These architectural visions are inseparable from the visions of architecture and the work of the visionary architects represented.

While the term "visionary" conjures up the idealistic, the Utopian, the impractical, and the dreamer, it has a much more positive side. It suggests a mental picture produced by the imagination. It suggests unusual perception into worlds we cannot visit everyday, except through the visual dramatization of that imaginative environment.

The art of architecture can also be said to have two meanings. It is the art and science of designing and constructing buildings, for certain; yet it also applies to any design or orderly arrangement of architectural forms and spaces, built or unbuilt.

There are also two meanings of the terms "imagination" and "imaginary," meaning unrealistic or fantasy on the one hand and the ability to deal creatively with an unseen reality on the other.

Even the Renaissance architect Piranesi thought twice about the difference. On the title plate for his well-known prison etchings, he had two versions. The first described them as "Imaginary Prisons." and the final second version as "Prisons of the Imagination."

Yet architectural fantasies like the prison series, which have endured for over three centuries, are among the creations of the mind that link yesterday with today and today with tomorrow. They infuse the present with a sense of the past and also give a glimpse of the future.

Visionary schemes are usually radically different from the concerns and icons of their day, and the artist or architect attempts to resolve these differences by means of transporting them into a hypothetical future environment. There are different types of visionary schemes; they may be based on social concerns, technological considerations, or new forms and materials.

Conceptual architecture, or architecture based on pure idea and imagination, often abandons the physical nature of architectural design. However, through a form of circular logic, these images may come even closer to the true meaning of architecture and design.

Some of the work in this collection is visionary indeed, as the authors of the works were students at the time and had not yet practiced architecture. They were able to explore the freedom of design and stretch their imagination to the fullest capacity, expressing their ideas without the rigors and restrictions of an architectural practice.

These unbuilt works of the imagination can be as influential on the future development of architectural form as projects that have been built. Many of the unbuilt works of the past are far more famous than their contemporary built counterparts. Even those that admittedly may have been better left unbuilt are still with us as a part of our architectural history.

Some of the work represented here has remained outside the mainstream of accepted architectural form, built or unbuilt, so this book corrects that omission. The material is presented in chronological order wherever possible. This is done not as a scholarly device, but as a guide in viewing the work in its relation to what we already know was the accepted architecture at the time. Much of the work is half a century old, or older, yet still has the appeal, the fascination to hold us even as we are now devising new forms for the future.

The complete history of architecture must include both the built environment and the unbuilt. For some projects, it may take a lifetime to realize completion; some may never reach that status for any number of reasons. Yet, they were all part of the fabric that has been woven by humanity around the globe for more than the last six millennia. This book deals primarily with the last three hundred years of that cycle.

V

Acknowledgments

This collection of work was assembled from many different sources, and I want to thank all those who participated in making the material available. Much of the historical works were obtained from galleries and museums, and I thank the many archivists of these institutions for their efforts in retrieving the documents, having them photographed in many instances, and sending them to me on a crash schedule. These sources are identified with their respective drawings on each page.

The following people were particularly helpful and instrumental in supplying reproductions for publication. John Rattenbury, Taliesin Architects, gave his early enthusiasm and encouragement to include the work of Frank Lloyd Wright from the Taliesin Foundation Archives, and thanks to Bruce Pfieffer of the Frank Lloyd Wright Foundation. A special thanks to Dennis Crompton for supplying material from the Archigram Archives. Also, I want to thank the many friends, artists and architects who supplied their own creative work for this book.

In addition, I thank my friend and editor of many years, Wendy Lochner, for her unyielding efforts to keep this project alive during a long development process, and through an equally longer production process. Tom Kowalczyk was extremely helpful in steering it through the final production and printing process.

Finally, a very special thanks to Joy, whose patience and understanding helped to ease the pressure of a deadline-oriented project spanning the better part of a year.

Table of Contents

Introduction

Ever since the first constructions for shelter, there have been those who have wanted to re-shape the world in which they lived. The architectural visions produced by these creative thinkers, environmentalists, high-tech enthusiasts, artists and other visionaries have always explored a world quite different from the mainstream. They have shown us new ways of living and working, and new aesthetic forms for building.

The concept behind this book was to display these creative approaches using both architectural projects and architectural art. It is meant to depict that which is outside the mainstream; the experimental, and the visionary.

The book is a compendium of images which communicates primarily on a visual level, without the distraction of text. Notes on the plates are in the back of the book. The format and page layout is designed to heighten this visual effect, as the pictures are large and full bleed wherever possible. Early attempts to depict architectural concepts and form are described in the text accompanying the first (and only) chapter. The work is then presented uninterrupted from the year 1 A.D. to the year 2000.

During the Renaissance, the representation of buildings grew rapidly, with the discovery of the principles of perspective. This new visualization tool also prompted experimentation with imaginary architectural scenes. Many architects and artists wrote extensively on the subject, while others expressed their ideas in drawings.

One Renaissance architect was particularly prolific, Giovanni Battista Piranesi, whose work remains revered to this day. Another was Guiseppe Bibiena, youngest of the Bibiena family of theatrical stage set designers. Joseph Michael Gandy represented the work of Europe's most noted architect, Sir John Soane, in imaginative drawings. Thomas Cole created romanticized hypothetical architectural scenes with his large scale paintings.

While there were many individual accomplishments on the visionary front along the way, there were periods of intense group activity, such as the work of the students at the Ecole des Beaux-Arts in Paris. The students produced imaginative large-scale hypothetical projects within the classical idioms of the day. Imagination was given a free reign, and their schemes were usually grandiose, and presented in extremely large, stunning watercolor drawings. It is interesting to compare the casino project by the student Louis-Hippolyte Boileau

in 1897, with the Wolf lake Amusement Park of Frank Lloyd Wright in 1895, on the following page.

Frank Lloyd Wright signaled the coming of a new age of design that broke with tradition on many fronts. This was expressed in his early designs for the Lake Tahoe project, the Gordon Strong Planetarium and the Doheny Ranch project. These represents some of the most imaginative early works of this master architect.

Meanwhile the young motion picture industry was having an impact on the architectural scene. The films *Metropolis* and *Just Imagine* introduced elaborate and imaginative architectural sets depicting futuristic scenes. These in turn influenced many artists and architects such as Hugh Ferriss and Raymond Hood, among others.

Walter Burleigh Griffen, a contemporary of Frank Lloyd Wright, was developing his own individualistic though somewhat similar style. Achilles Rizzoli, an architect in San Francisco, was producing imaginative and beautiful delineations of work borne out of interpretations of his own introspective experiences. Another bay area architect, Bernard Maybeck, who had designed the Palace of Fine Arts for the 1916 Pan Pacific Exposition, later produced many other innovative structures.

The Russian architect Iakov Chernikov experimented with abstract architectural form in bold compositions of building masses. He may have been the first to publish his belief that developing the imagination was a way to discover true architectural expression.

Frank Lloyd Wright was now in his second major career phase, designing notable large scale projects, some of which were self-initiated. They remained unbuilt, but that did not deter him from producing a prodigious amount of future work.

Some of the most imaginative and unusual work came from mid-western architect Bruce Goff. Rather than imitate or be influenced by other architects he chose instead to develop his own individualistic approach based on the wishes and needs of each individual client. Therefore no two structures ever resembled one another. Modern music and objects from nature were also influential on his work.

He also developed an approach to teaching that was based on design principals related to music, and transferred that approach to students over the period of a decade. The resultant student work was the most imaginative ever produced by students anywhere. Many of those projects are published here for the first time since they were produced nearly half a century ago. They cover the years from 1950 to 1959, and highlight the work of many of the author's classmates, as well as his own work. They include works by Joseph Wythe, Herb Greene, Howard Alan, James Gardner, Dale Camacho, Robert Faust, Jack Golden, James Gresham, Arthur Kohara, Jacques Gillet, and John Hurtig.

Frank Lloyd Wright continued to produce many notable and imaginative projects. Among them a design for the Arizona State capital, which he self-initiated, and many plans and sketches for the Broadacre City Project, which would span nearly two decades. Here, large scale buildings were treated as artifacts in a wide open and consciously designed landscape. Another self-initiated project, Monona Terrace in Madison Wisconsin would be realized nearly 60 years later, by the Taliesin Architects.

In London, Peter Cook organized and led the group Archigram for over a decade, which included Ron Herron and others. Peter Cook's *Plug-in City* and Ron Herron's *Walking City* are prime examples of expandable and constantly evolving structures. *Plug-in City* was indeed a megastructure that could be constantly changed, while Ron Herron's *Walking Cities* was a collection of self-contained structures that were adaptable to a variety of environments.

Paolo Soleri had a totally opposite approach. He viewed a landscape where a hundred acres was needed to do the work of one, and as a result developed his concept of miniaturization. Soleri's structures have often been mislabeled as mega-structures, when in reality they were condensed communities for living, working and recreation combined into a single organic environment.

Bruce Goff and Frank Lloyd Wright's teachings have been assimilated into the innovative work of Arthur Dyson, now Dean of the Taliesin School of Architecture.

Eugene Tsui, developed his own philosophy called "Evolutionary Architecture", which is based on principals found in nature.

Artist Syd Mead produced many imaginative futuristic illustrations for commercial, industrial, and film use. His background paintings for the film BladeRunner are legendary.

Architect Stanley Tigerman produced playful and imaginative sketches, which were in reality studies in architectural form. Architect Harvey Ferraro's designs stem from his studies with Bruce Goff, plus his own unique transformation of forms. Albert Lorenz developed an imaginative style of Illustration, representing architectural environments

in both traditional perspective layouts, and using his own curved perspective projection system.

Architect Arthur Cotton Moore turned to paintings, whose free forms crept back into the details on his imaginative buildings. Architect James Rossant's series of "Cities in the Sky" are perhaps the most unique combination of building forms set into a fantastic grid .

Nancy Wolf's artistic visions and parodies of architectural facades and follies are insightful criticisms into a world that made strangers out of its occupants. Architect Tad Berezowski expressed his vision with a series of imaginary towers and imaginary villas, executed as very large drawings. Visionary architect Paul Laffoly's paintings are explorations into the world of the metaphysical.

Many architects have turned to architectural drawing for their exercises into the world of imagination, such as Frank Costantino and Jeffrey George, Ian McKay, Manual Avila, Gilbert Gorski, Richard Ferrier, Gordon Grice, Christopher Grubbs, James Akers, artist Douglas Cooper, Ron Love, Lori Brown and the late Robert McIlhargey,

Thomas Shaller, architect and author, is well known for his watercolor paintings of imaginary environments, as well as his traditional renderings. Architect Kevin Woest takes a new look at an old concept; using bridge structures as habitats. Ernest burden, III created a series of drawings fashioned after Piranesi's prisons.

Since a new millennium is upon us, and science and technology is shaping our future, a new generation of artists and architects are developing virtual forms that seem to have emerged from a fantasyland. Stephan Hoffpauir's *Sony Station* and Hans-Christian Lischewski's *Cybercities* is an example. This new architecture with spaces that warp and forms that twist, represents a new experimentation with architectural form using 3D computer-generated designs. The interiors of these amorphous new structures, whose curved walls merge seamlessly into floors and ceilings, offer a new hope that the era of the grid is dead. It is now giving way to new forms of expression, including fractels, folds, and waves. At this time we see the future, and it is curved.

Finally, the world of film is once again providing the impetus for the visionary imagery. Advanced computer-generated special effects are depicting visionary environments that we can visit only in our imaginations.

Chapter One: Precedents and Architectural Visions 1-2000

Although the birth of art may extend 35 millennia into our past, architectural subjects as artistic expression did not come into prominence until roughly the first century A. D., give or take a few hundred years.

It is obvious from records of cave art that the primary focus was survival, which was reflected in the drawings of the animals that sustained them.

Early civilizations of the Near East also depicted animals, figures, warriors and even chariots in their art. Bas-relief sculptures were common in this essentially mud brick civilization. The famed Ishtar Gate was faced with glazed bricks, with relief figures of various animals. At Persepolis, the representations included figures battling with lions or in processions.

In Egyptian art, although some papyrus has been found that contained plans of temple shrines, the representation on temple walls and in tombs did not include architectural features.

In early Cretan art, murals and frescoes featured the human figure, even landscapes, but lacked any representation of architectural forms. Greek art mastered the human figure, both in painted form on pottery and in free-standing sculpture, and as bas-relief friezes on buildings. It was perhaps Etruscan art that broke the barriers, wherein walls were decorated with household scenes and utensils, yet even here architectural forms were missing.

The progression from flat to spatial wall decoration was discovered to have existed in houses buried for centuries under the ashes in Pompeii and Herculaneum. The discovered artworks were categorized into four successive but overlapping styles. The first, appearing around 200-60 B.C., divided the wall into bright polychrome panels of solid colors with occaisional schematically rendered contrasting textures. The style was called "incrustation."

A wall painting from the Villa Boscoreale near Pompeii (see illustration, opposite) shows the second style, aptly named "architectural," which dates to around 20-60 A. D. Here, the decoration is no longer restricted to a single visual plane. The space of the room is made to look as if it extends beyond the room itself by the representation of architectural forms in a visually convincing but not

systematic method of perspective. Columns, pilasters, and window frames painted on the wall serve to frame distant views of other structures, furniture and landscaping.

This is an unusual representation in that the lines of perspective projection do not converge to a single vanishing point on the horizon, as in later Renaissance perspective. Instead, several vanishing points with associated converging lines are distributed on an axis that runs vertically through the center of the panel.

By the fifth century, architectural elements were used as backdrops in the proliferation of religious art that would capture and hold all art throughout Europe for centuries.

The architectural visions of the Middle Ages exist as scant literary records only, so there is not much that can be learned from them. By the mid fourteenth century woodcuts and etchings gave us a clue of medieval towns, but the method of representation was somewhat abstract

In the middle of the sixteenth century, a Dutch painter-turned-architect, Jan Vredeman de Vries, produced numerous engravings in which he opened new avenues of architectural representation and invention. His works were pure fantasy, but regarded as avante-garde messages in the depiction of architectural space. His greatest contribution was his treatise on the rules of perspective, which, however, were not new by this time. They had already been formulated in the fifteenth century by Piero Della Francesca and Leon Battista Alberti, among others. They had been further refined in the sixteenth century by Serlio and Vignola and they were thoroughly familiar to Leonardo, Raphael, and all the Italian master painters.

However, this new method of depicting architectural space and form in true perspective spurred experimentations in architectural visions on every level. Architects and painters alike were now free to let their imaginations soar. The images on the pages that follow are their story, depicted in chronological order.

Wall Painting: (Opposite) From the cubiculum of the Villa Boscoreale, near Pompei.
Courtesy of The Metropolitan Museum, New York City

1

3

8 Preceding page: **Giovanni Battista Piranesi** Architectural Fantasy (Etching, 1735) (Courtesy of The Morgan Library, New York C

Giuseppe Galli Bibiena Theatrical Stage Design, (Engraving, ca. 1740) 9

12　**Joseph Michael Gandy** Sir John Soane's Public and Private Buildings (Watercolor, 1818)

13

Emmaneul Brune Principal Staircase of the Palace of a Sovereign (Watercolor, 1863)

18 **Erastus Salisbury Field** Historical Monument of the American Republic (Oil on canvas, 1876)

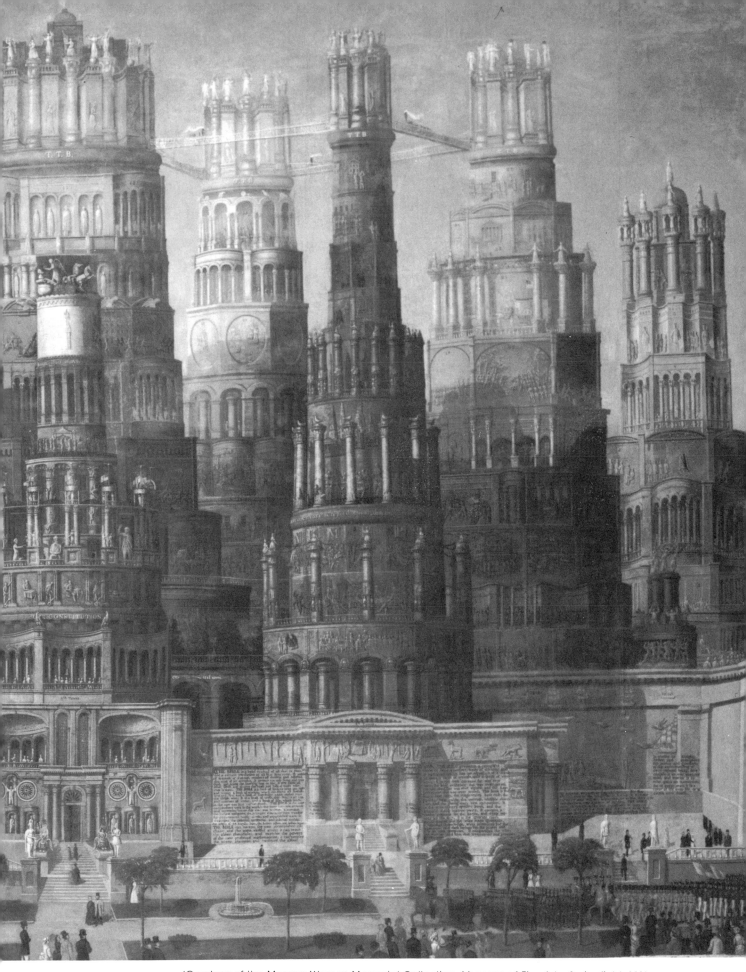

19

Louis-Hippolyte Boileau Casino (Watercolor, 1897)

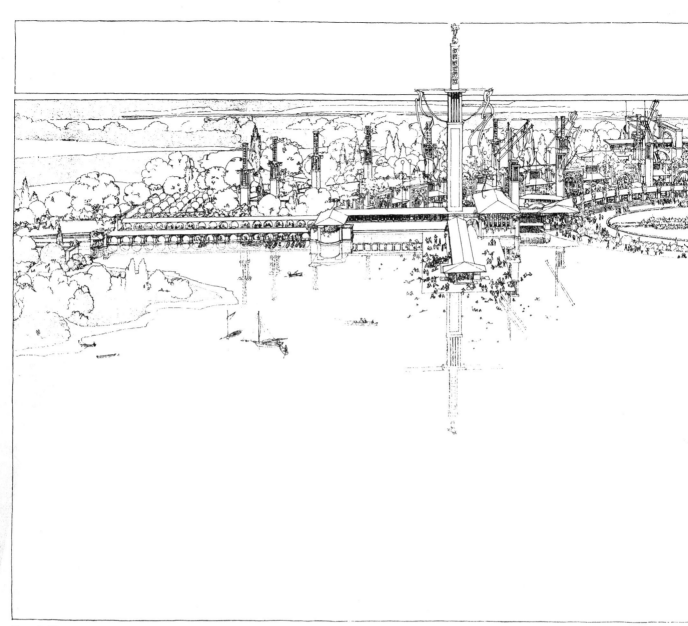

Frank Lloyd Wright Wolf Lake Amusement Park (Ink line on paper 1895)

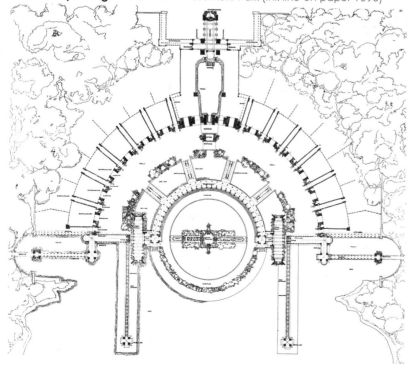

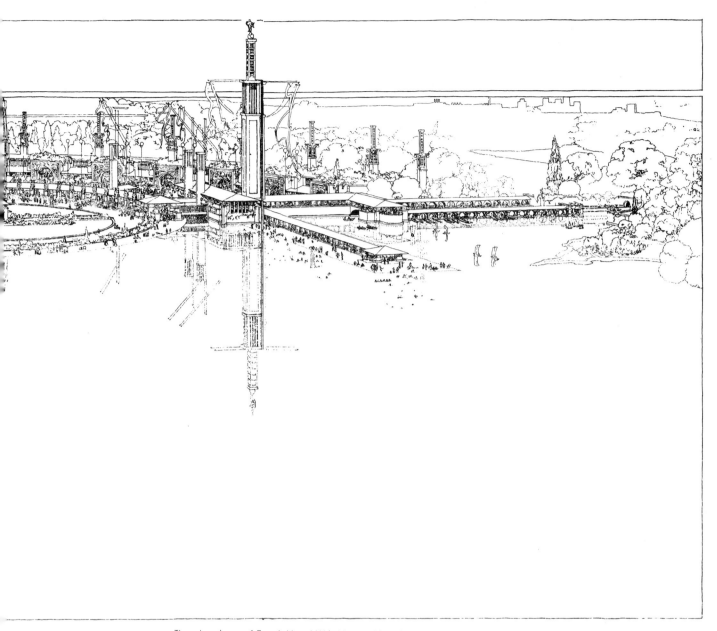

Frank Lloyd Wright Lake Tahoe Summer Colony: Perspective (Colored pencil, 1922)

Frank Lloyd Wright Gordon Strong Planetarium (Pencil, 1924)
The drawings of Frank Lloyd Wright are Copyright © 1999 The Frank Lloyd Wright Foundation, Scottsdale

Frank Lloyd Wright Doheny Ranch Resort: Perspective (Colored pencil, 1923)

The drawings of Frank Lloyd Wright are Copyright © 1999 The Frank Lloyd wright Foundation, Scottsdale

Raymond Hood Apartments on a Bridge. Rendering by Hugh Ferriss (Pencil, 1929)
(Courtesy of Avery Architectural Archives, Columbia University, New York)

Joseph D. Murphy Restaurant in the Air, Beaux Arts Competition (Watercolor, 1929)
(Courtesy of MIT School of Architecture Museum)

METROPOLIS Still scene from the movie. (1928) (Courtesy of Photofest, New York City)

JUST IMAGINE Still scene from the film (1929) (Courtesy of Photofest, New York City)

Hugh Ferriss Isolated Masses: (Pencil on tracing paper, 1931) (Courtesy of Avery Drawings and Archives, Columbia University, New York)

Preceding page: **Entrance** Civic and Business Center of Meadow City, New Jersey (Ink on paper, 1930)
(Courtesy of Regional Plan Association of New York)

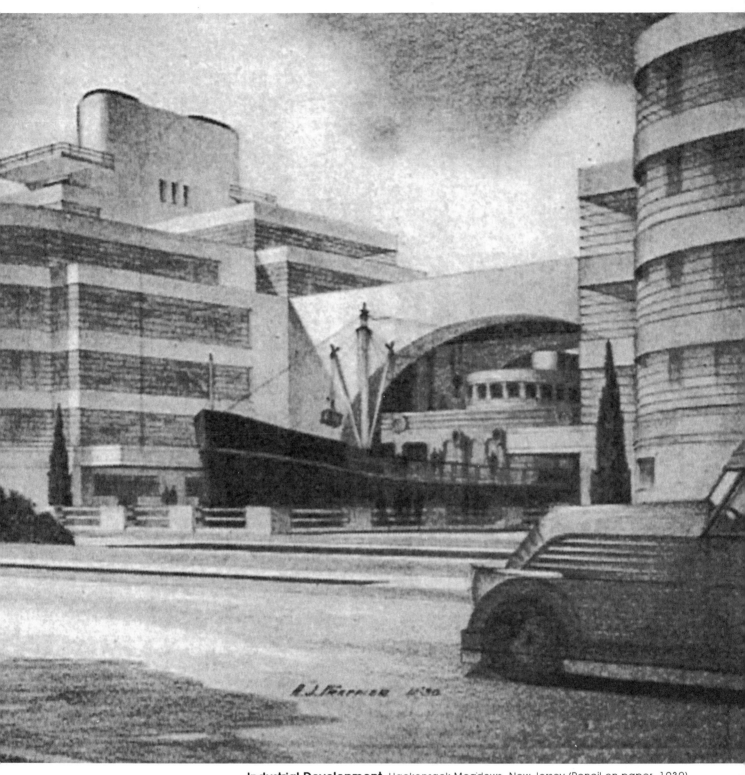

Industrial Development Hackensack Meadows, New Jersey (Pencil on paper, 1930)
(Courtesy of Regional Plan Association of New York)

40   **E. Maxwell Fry**   Future Tower City (Ink on paper, 1932) (Courtesy of Regional Plan Association of New York)

Proposed Christie – Forsyth Parkway (Pencil, 1932) (Courtesy of Regional Plan Association of New York City)

Ralph T. Walker Tower of Water and Light for the Chicago 1933 Exposition (Pencil on paper, 1932) (Courtesy of Regional Plan Association of New York)

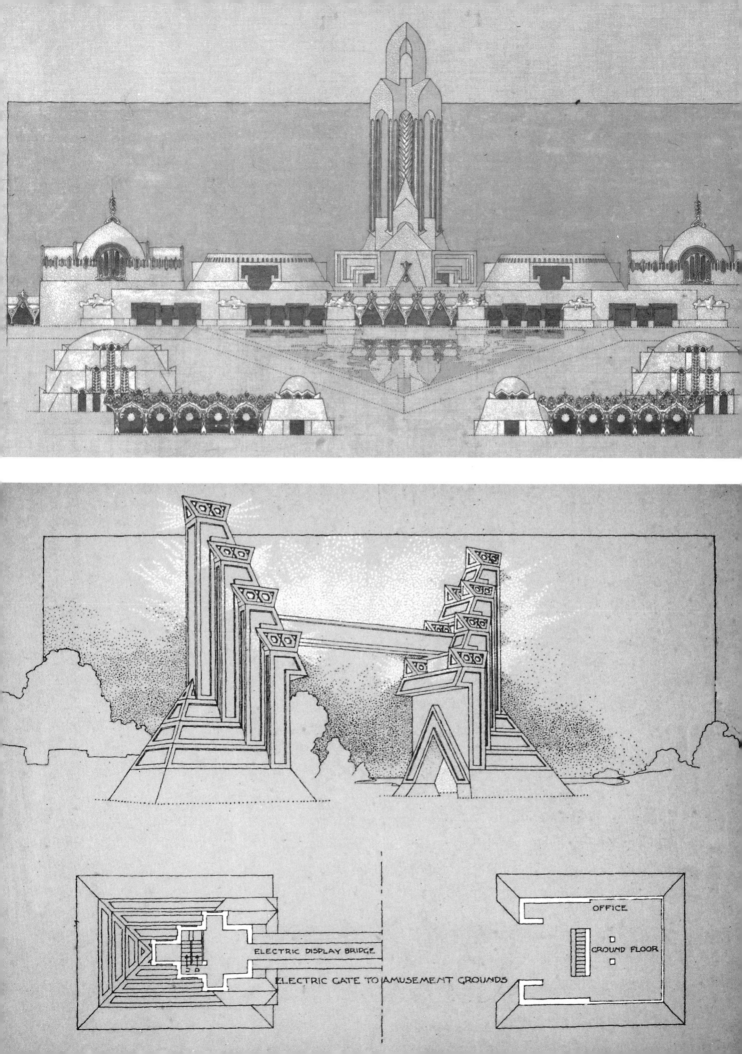

ELECTRIC DISPLAY BRIDGE

ELECTRIC GATE TO AMUSEMENT GROUNDS

OFFICE

GROUND FLOOR

Walter Burley Griffen Elevation: United Provinces Exhibition of Industry and Agriculture, Lucknow, India (Ink on cloth, 1935)
Below: Electric Gate to the Amusement Grounds: (Ink on colored paper, 1935)
(Courtesy of Avery Drawings and Archives, Columbia University, New York)

46   **Hugh Ferriss** New York World's Fair (Crayon on paper, 1936)

TO SHATTER THE ISOLATIONS TO

INFORMATIO

BOARD OF DESIGN 19

48   **Achilles G. Rizzoli** Janet M. Peck Painted Pictorially (Ink on rag paper, 1936)

SAYS SHE JU UBLFT PME SPNBO CMPPE
UP JOTUJUVUF UIF FYRVJTJUF

LOVE'S
DELIGHTFUL
LABORS

COMMUNICATO

DELLA VISTA DOLORES

49

Achilles G. Rizzoli Mother Symbolically Represented (Ink on rag paper, 1937)

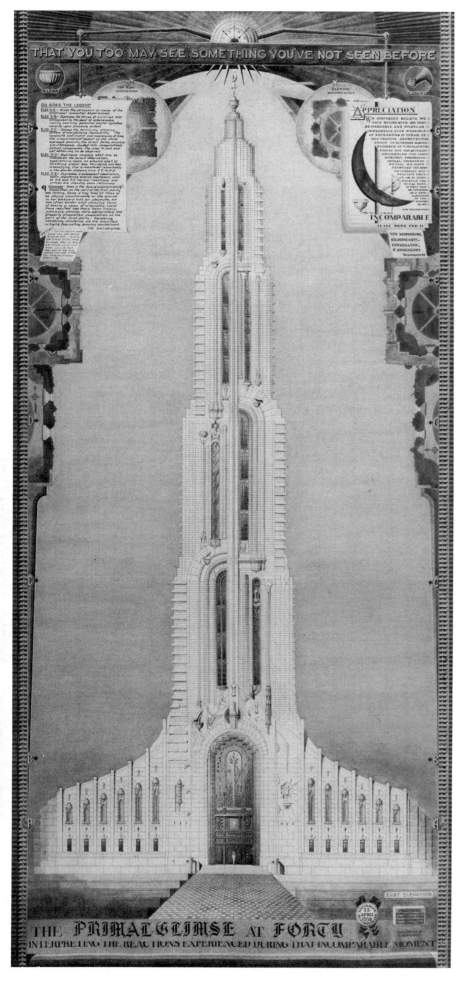

Achilles G. Rizzoli The Primalglimse at Forty
(Ink on rag paper, 1938)
(Courtesy of the Ames Gallery, Berkeley, California)

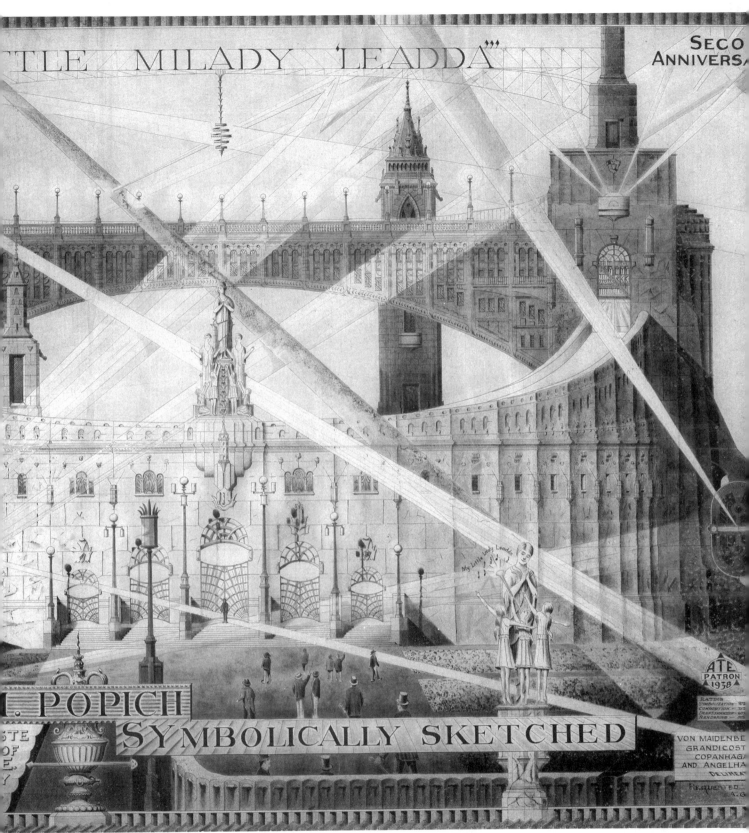

Achilles G. Rizzoli Grace M. Popich Symbolically Sketched (Ink on rag paper, 1938)
(Courtesy of the Collection of Dr. Siri von Reis)

54   **Bernard Maybeck** Music Temple, Golden Gate Exposition, San Francisco (1939)

55

Iakov Georgievich Chernikov Compositional Invention of Diverse Volumes with Decorative Coloring (Ink, 1933)
(Courtesy Collection Centre Canadien d'Architecture / Canadian Centre for Architecture, Montreal.)

J. Caponneto Suggested Display by Gardner Displays for the New York World's Fair (Tempera on black board, 1938)
(Courtesy of Museum of the City of New York)

THINGS TO COME Still image from the film (1939) (Courtesy Museum of Modern Art Film Still Archives, New York City) 57

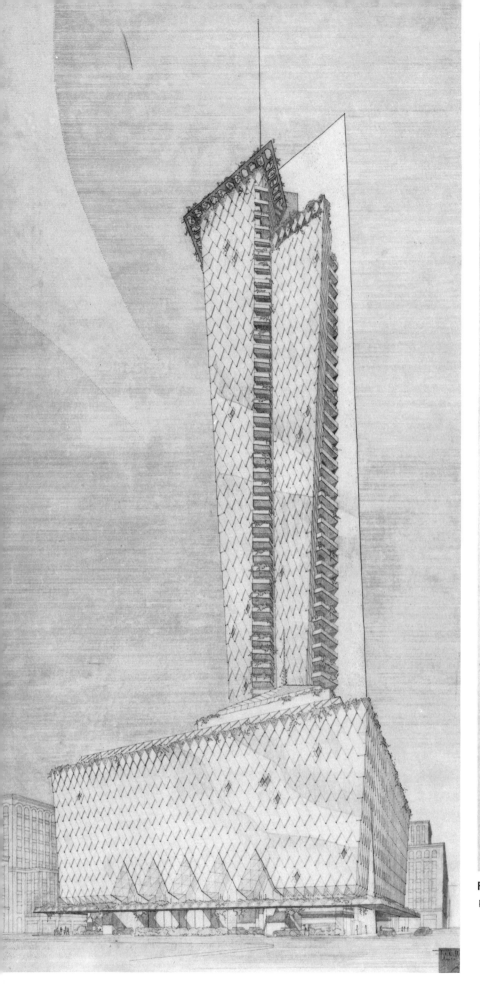

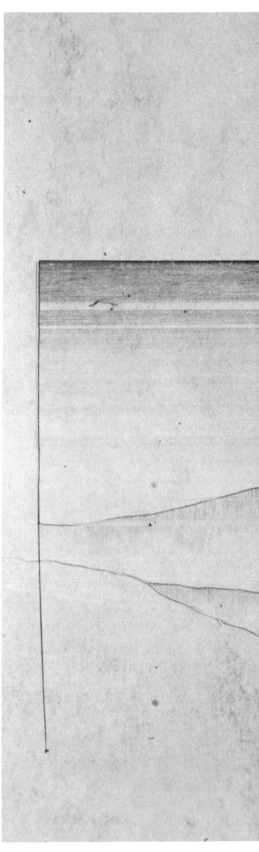

Frank Lloyd Wright Roger Lacey Hotel:
Perspective (Ink and pencil, 1946)

Frank Lloyd Wright Huntington Hartford Resort (Colored pencil, 1947)

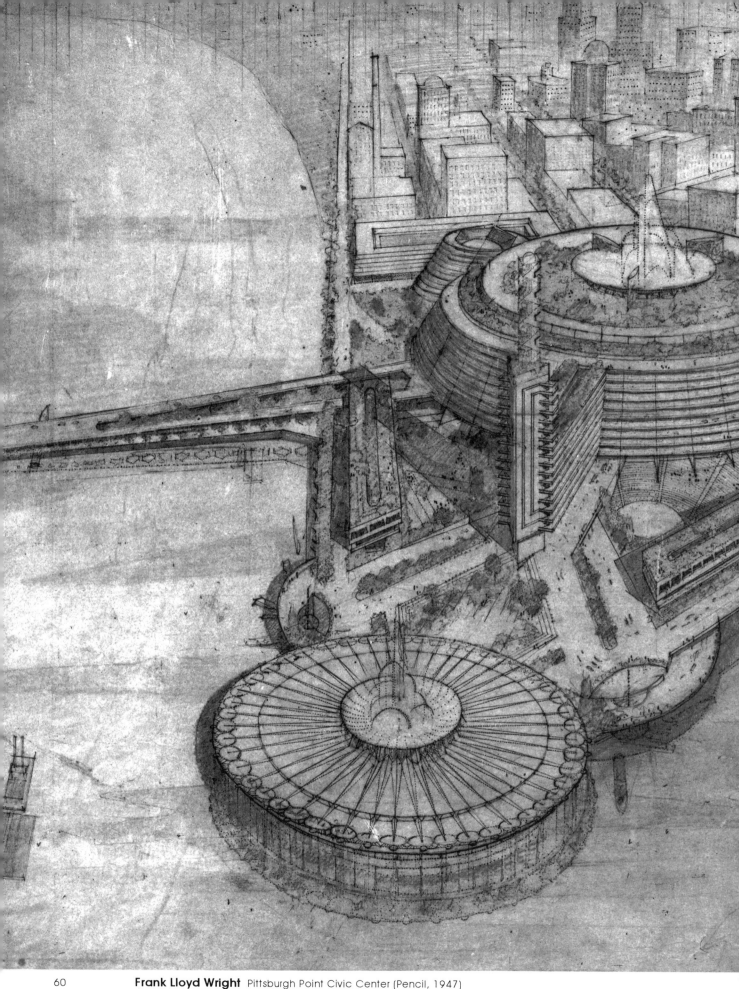

Frank Lloyd Wright Pittsburgh Point Civic Center (Pencil, 1947)

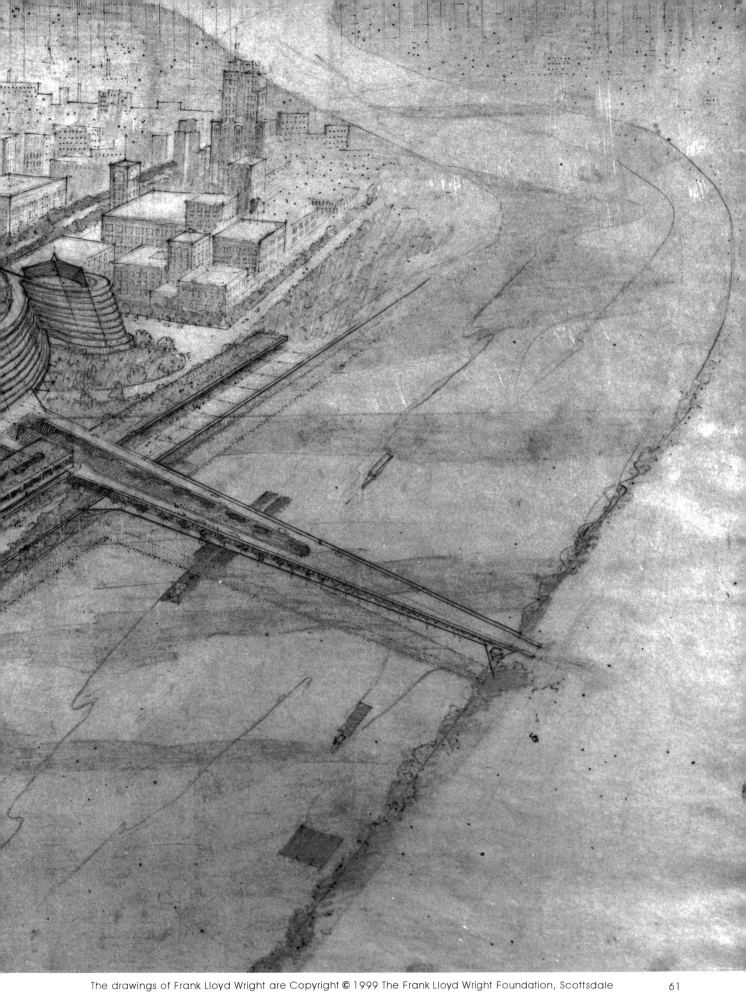

61

Frank Lloyd Wright Twin Cantilevered Bridges: (Night Perspective, 1947)

Bruce Alonzo Goff, American, 1904-1982, John Garvey House number 1: Aerial perspective, delineated by Herb Greene, American, b.1929, Graphite on white tracing paper, 1952, 71 x 90.6 cm, Gift of Shin'enKan, Inc., 1990.860.1 (Courtesy of The Art Institute of Chicago)

Bruce Alonzo Goff, American, 1904-1982, Joe Price Studio number 1, Perspective view, Pencil and colored pencil on tracing paper, 1953, 68.5 x 109 cm, Gift of Shin'enKan, Inc., 1990.859.1 (Courtesy of The Art Institute of Chicago)

68   **Bruce Alonzo Goff** American, 1904-1982, Ignacio Perez House number 2: Perspective from below

print on paper, 1954, 70.6 x 99.7 cm, Gift of Shin'enKan, Inc., RX 18410.54.07.6 (Courtesy of The Art Institute of Chicago)   69

Joseph Wythe Eagle Nest (Ink line and tone drawing on board, 1948)

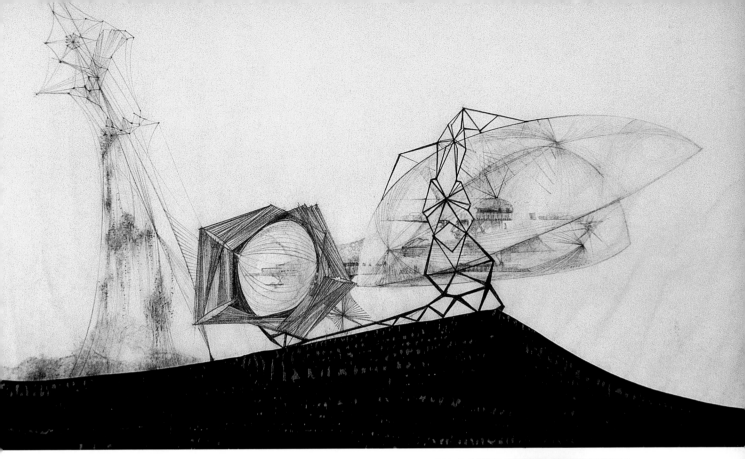

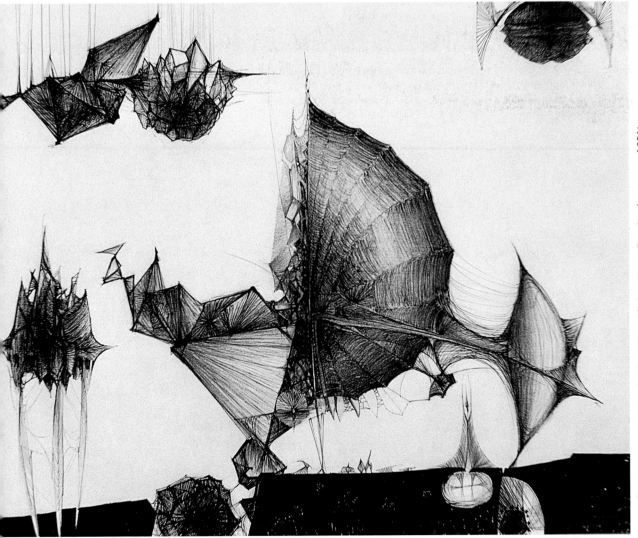

Robert Faust Top: Study in Architectural Character; Aspiration (Colored pencil on tracing paper, 1953)
Bottom: Service Station (Colored pencil on tracing paper, 1953)
Right: Study in Architectural Form; Reflection (Colored pencil on tracing paper, 1954)
Following page: Study in Architectural Form; Transparency (Colored pencil on tracing paper, 1954)

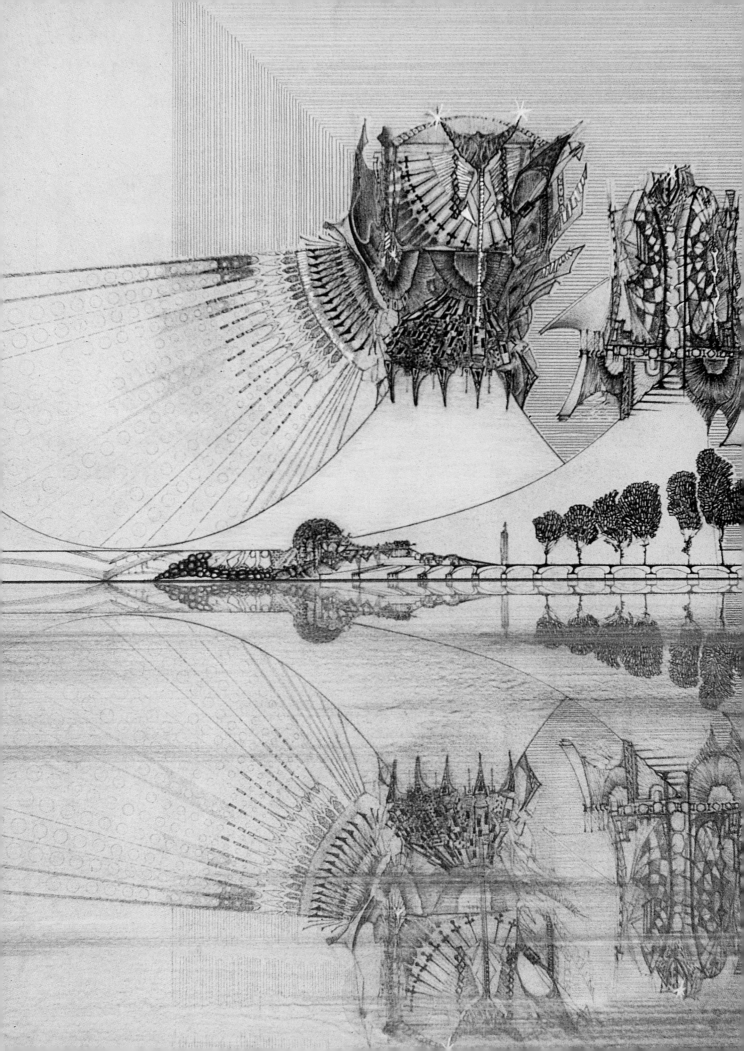

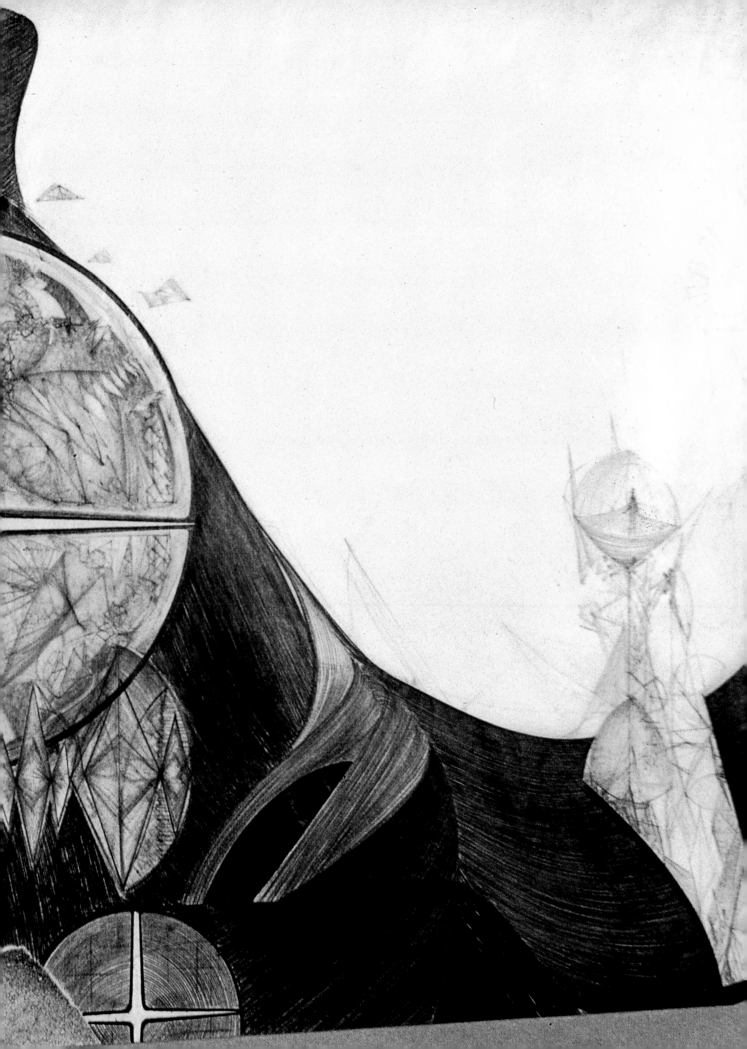

Ernest Burden Above: Studies in Architectural Form; Transparency. Right: Simplicity (Colored pencil on tracing paper, 1955)

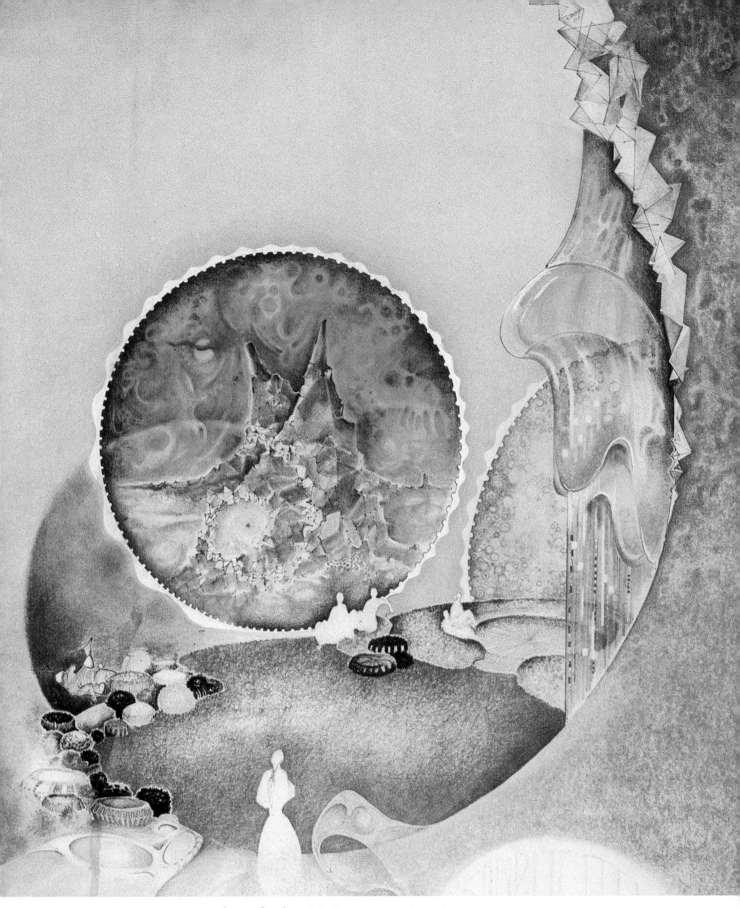

James Gardner Following page: Study in Architectural Form (Colored pencil on tracing paper, 1953)

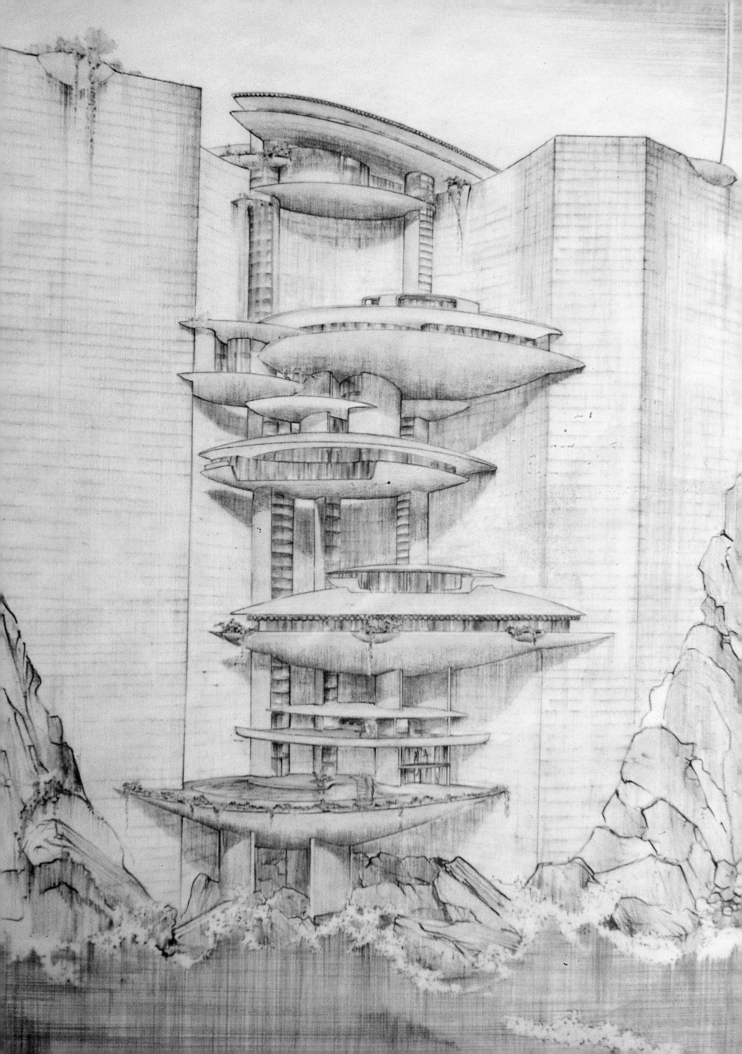

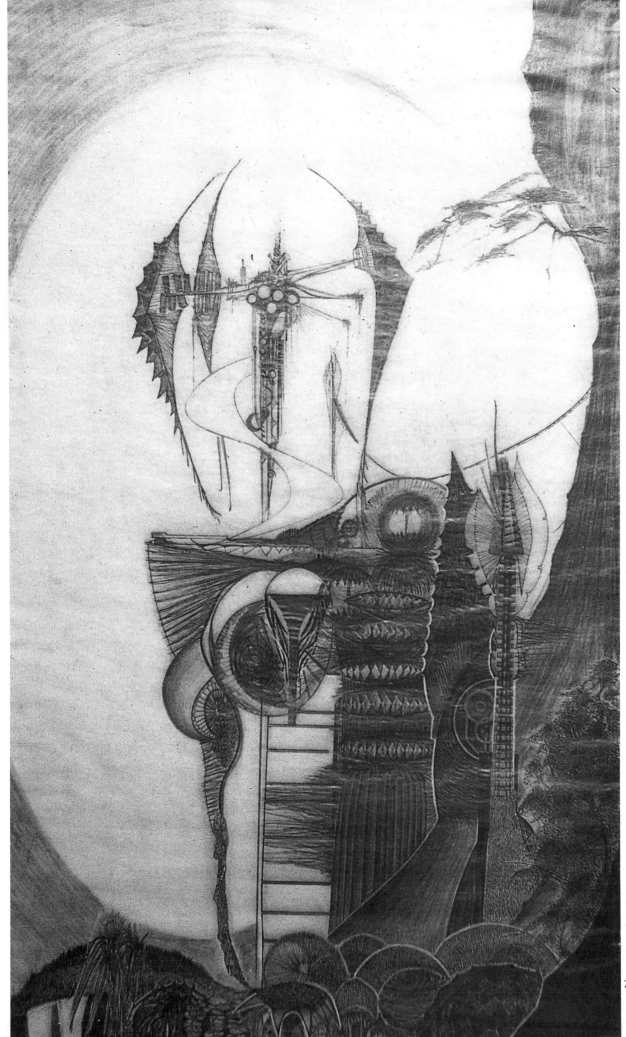

Robert Faust Incident, Terminal Climax (Black pencil on tracing paper, 1954) Following Page: **Howard Alan** Architectural Composition (Ink line sepia print, 1953)

Robert Faust Top: House for an Introvert (Black pencil on tracing paper, 1954)

Bottom: Study in Site Relationship; Contrasting (Black Pencil on tracing paper, 1954)

Above: Study in Architectural Form: Orchestration of Materials (Black Pencil on tracing paper, 1954)

A STUDY IN
PROPORTION
TRANSPARENCY
TRANSLUCENCY
OPACITY

THEME

VARIATION & DEVELOPMENT

Ernest Burden Top: Study in Proportion (Colored pencil, 1956) Bottom: Theme, Variation, Development (Pencil, 1956) Right: Study in Architectural Form and Balance (Ink, 1956)

Ernest Burden Top: Reflection (Pencil on tracing paper, 1955) Bottom: Architectural Sketch (Ink on paper, 1955)

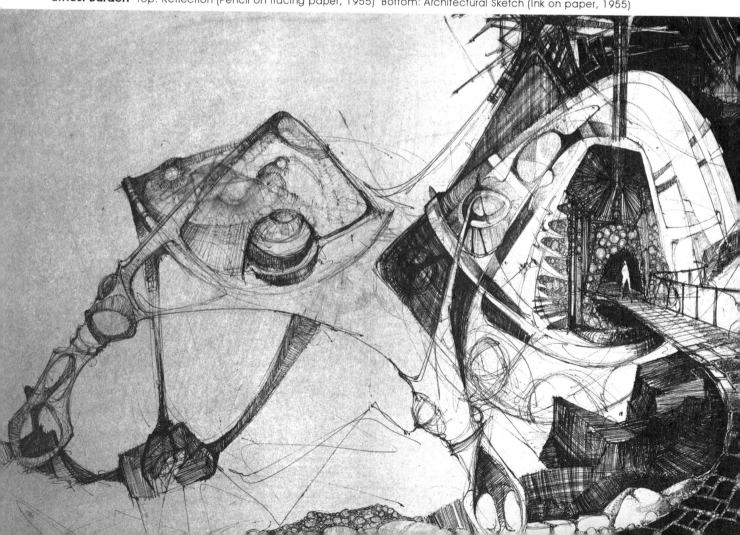

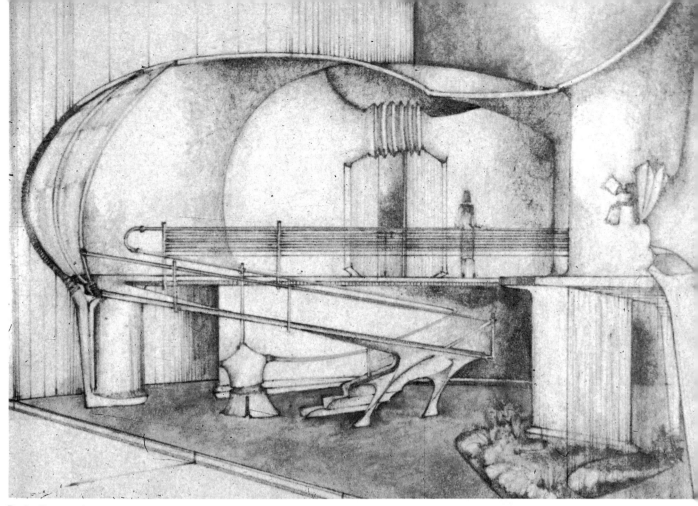

Dale Camacho Studies in Architectural Form (Pencil on board, 1956

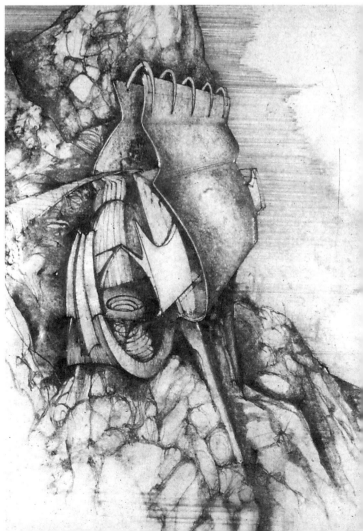

Student Drawing University of Oklahoma: Top, Bottom, Bottom Right: Studies in Architectural Form (Ink, 1956)

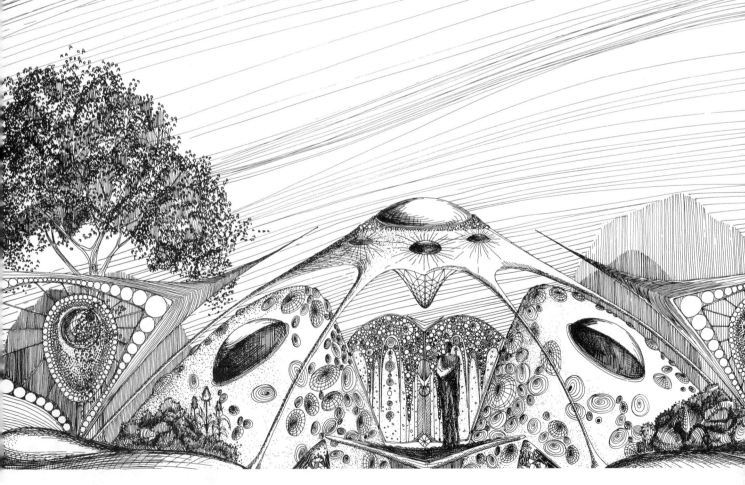

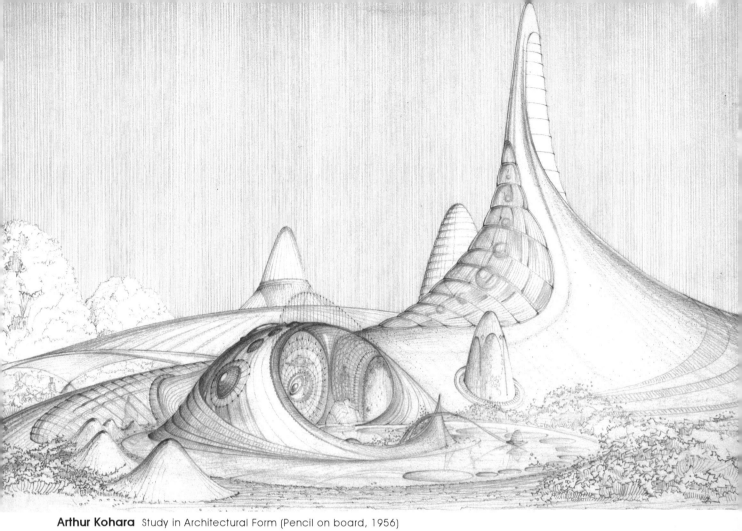

Arthur Kohara Study in Architectural Form (Pencil on board, 1956)

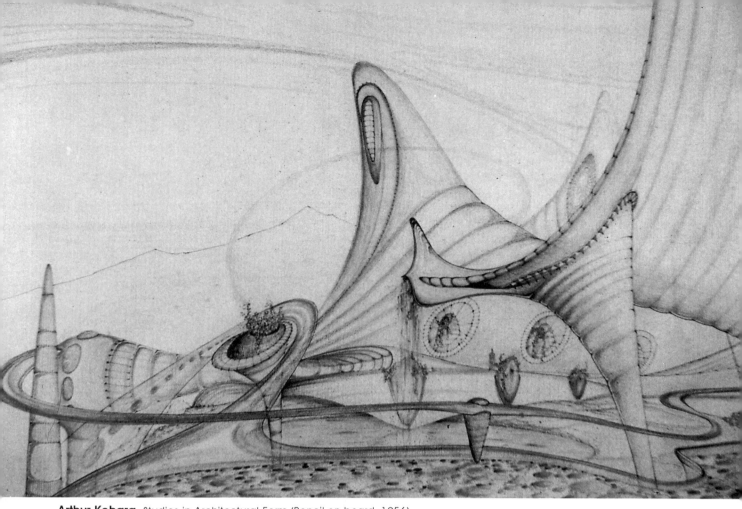

Arthur Kohara Studies in Architectural Form (Pencil on board, 1956)

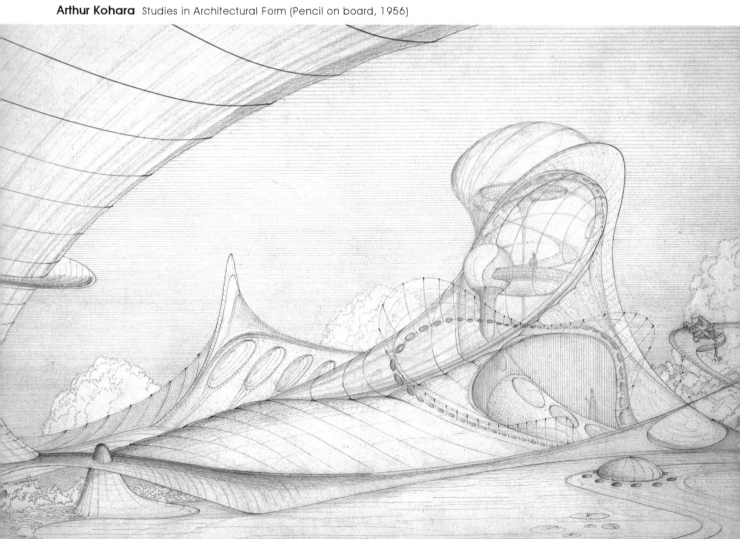

Arthur Kohara Studies in Architectural Form (Pencil on board, 1956)

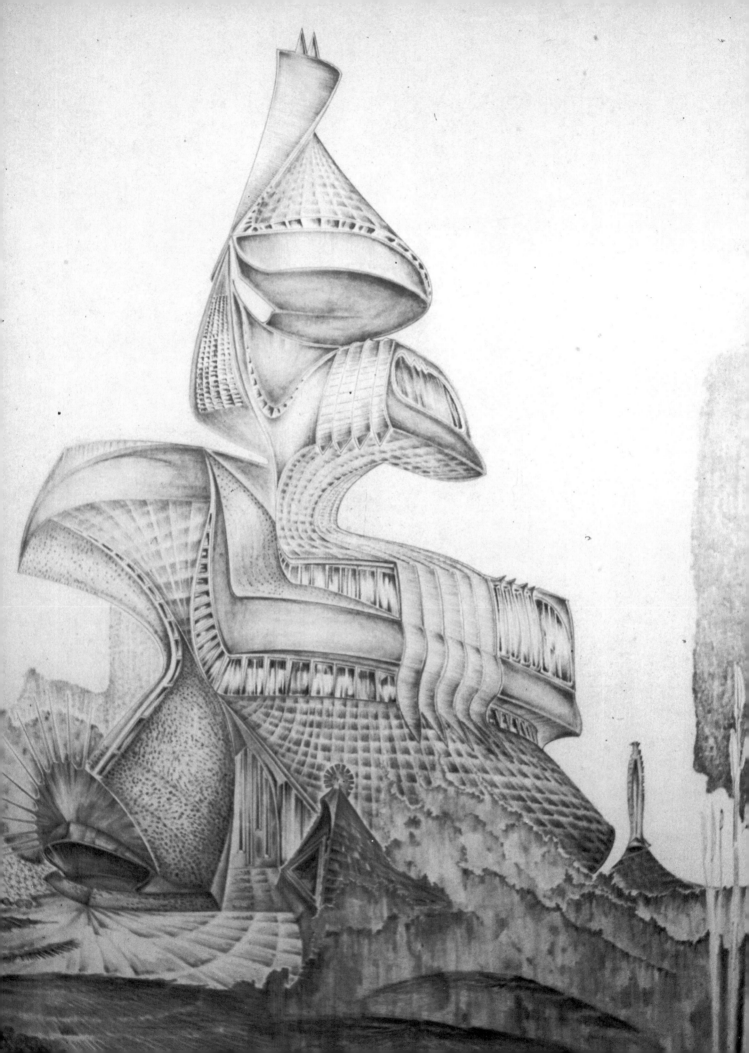

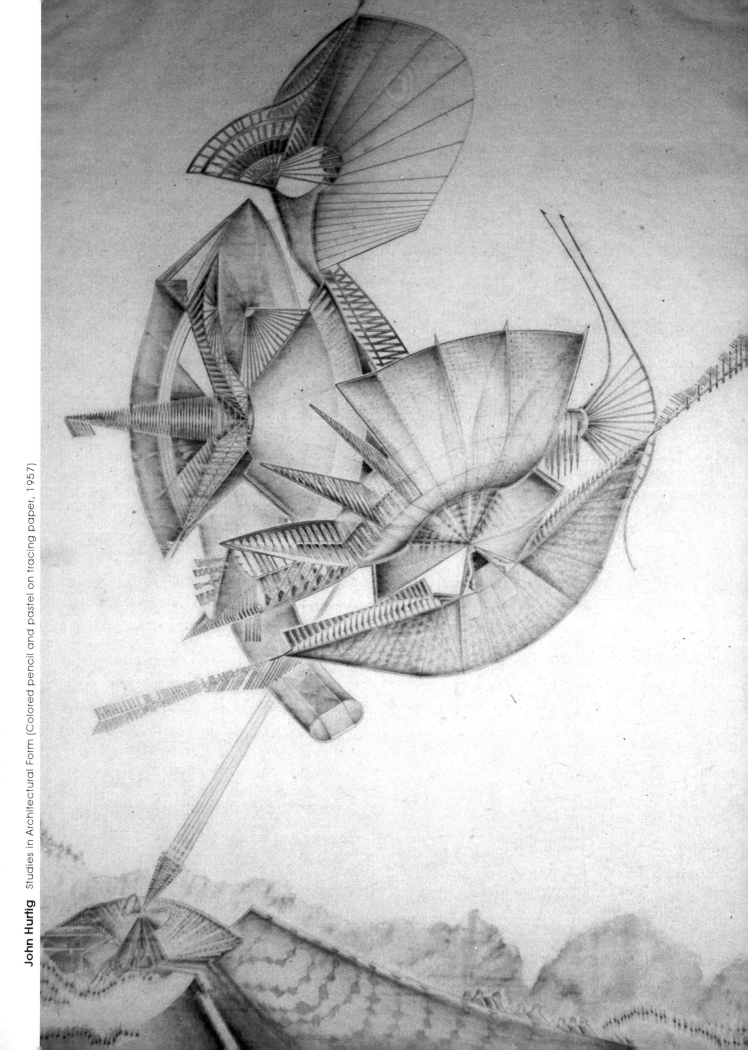

John Hurtig Studies in Architectural Form (Colored pencil and pastel on tracing paper, 1957)

John Hurtig Study in Architectural Form (Colored pencil and pastel on tracing paper, 1957)

Jack Golden Aviary/Aquarium (Pencil, 1956) Top Right: Zoo (Pencil, 1956) Bottom Right: Restaurant (Pencil, 1956)

Jack Golden Study in Architectural Form: Smooth Modulation (Pencil on tracing paper, 1956)

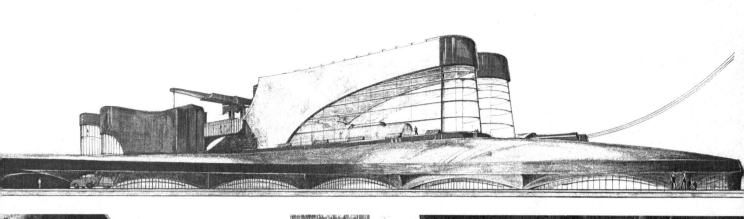

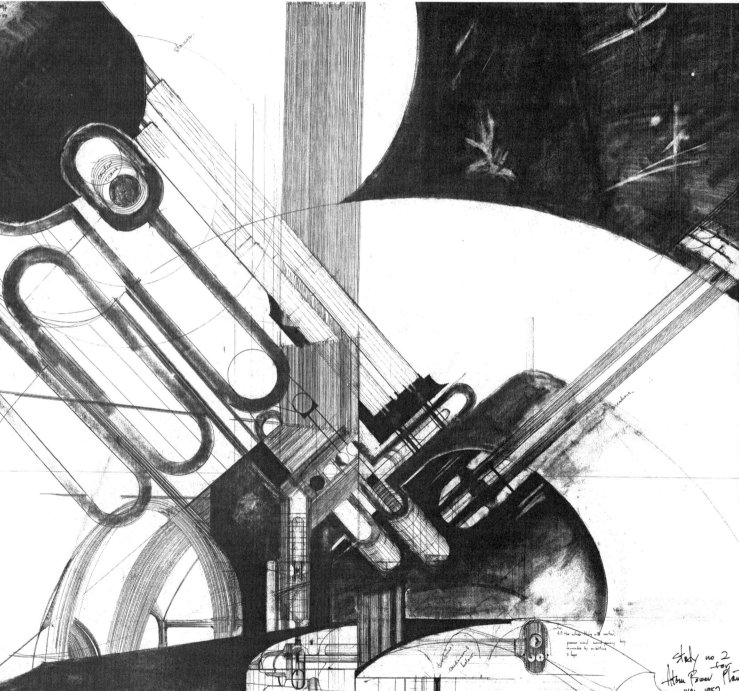

Howard Alan Top Left: Study in Architectural Form: Counterpoint (Pencil on tracing paper, 1957)
Howard Alan   Bottom Left: Study in Architectural Form: Irregular Rhythm (Pencil on tracing paper, 1957)
Howard Alan Above: Atomic Power Plant (Pencil on tracing paper, 1957)

103

James Gresham Residence (Pencil on tracing paper, 1957)

PRO BONO PUBLICO · ARIZONA ·

FRANK LLOYD WRIGHT ARCHITECT
FEBRUARY 17. 1957

Frank Lloyd Wright Arizona State Capital: Aerial Perspective (Colored pencil 1957)

107

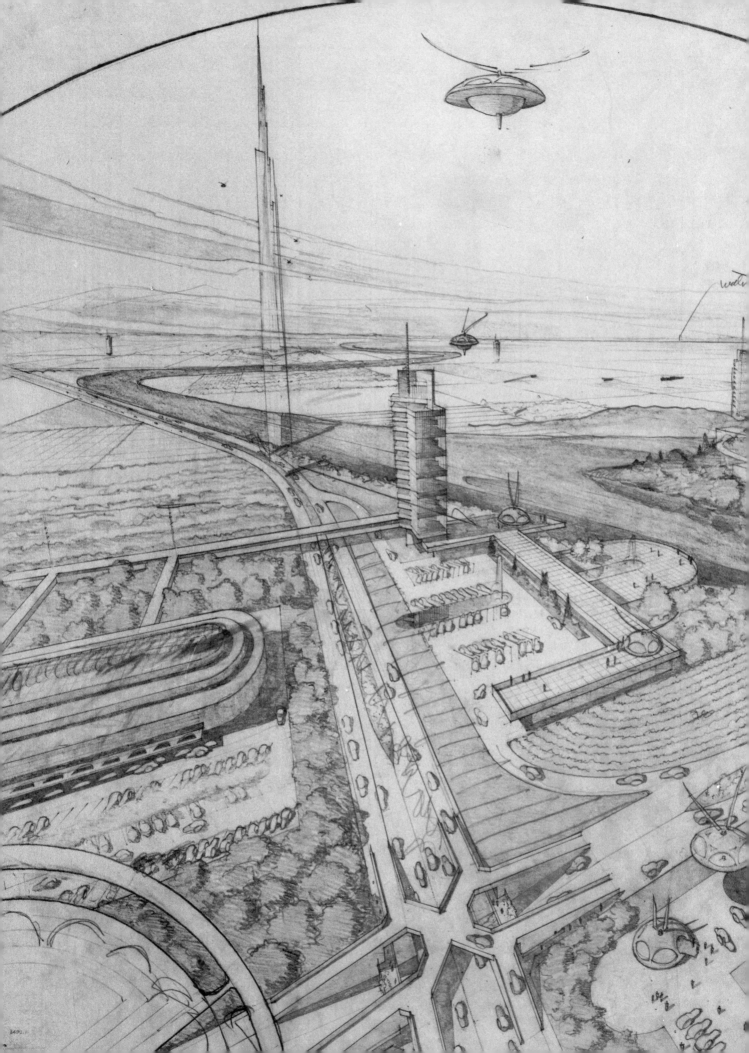

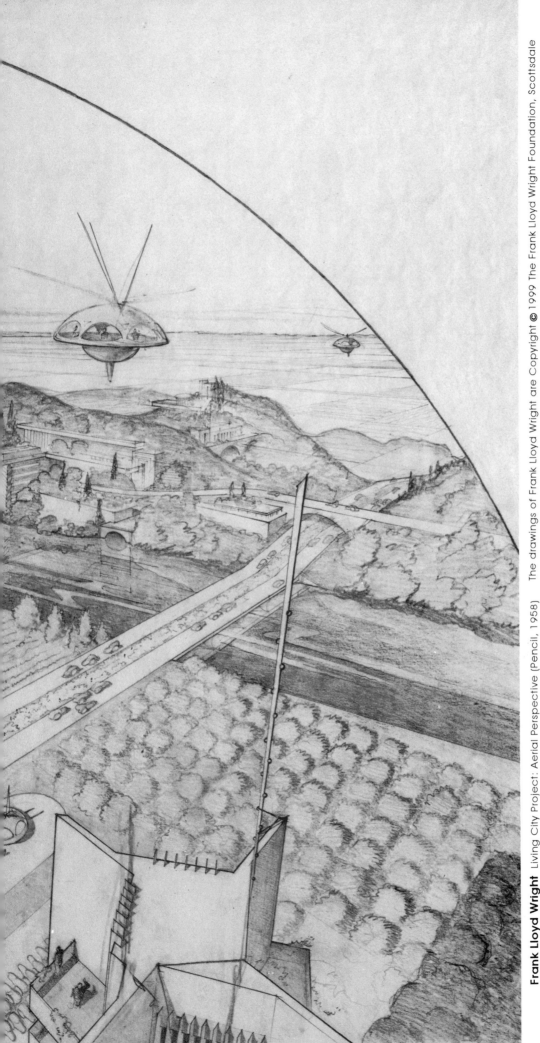

Frank Lloyd Wright Living City Project: Aerial Perspective (Pencil, 1958)   The drawings of Frank Lloyd Wright are Copyright © 1999 The Frank Lloyd Wright Foundation, Scottsdale

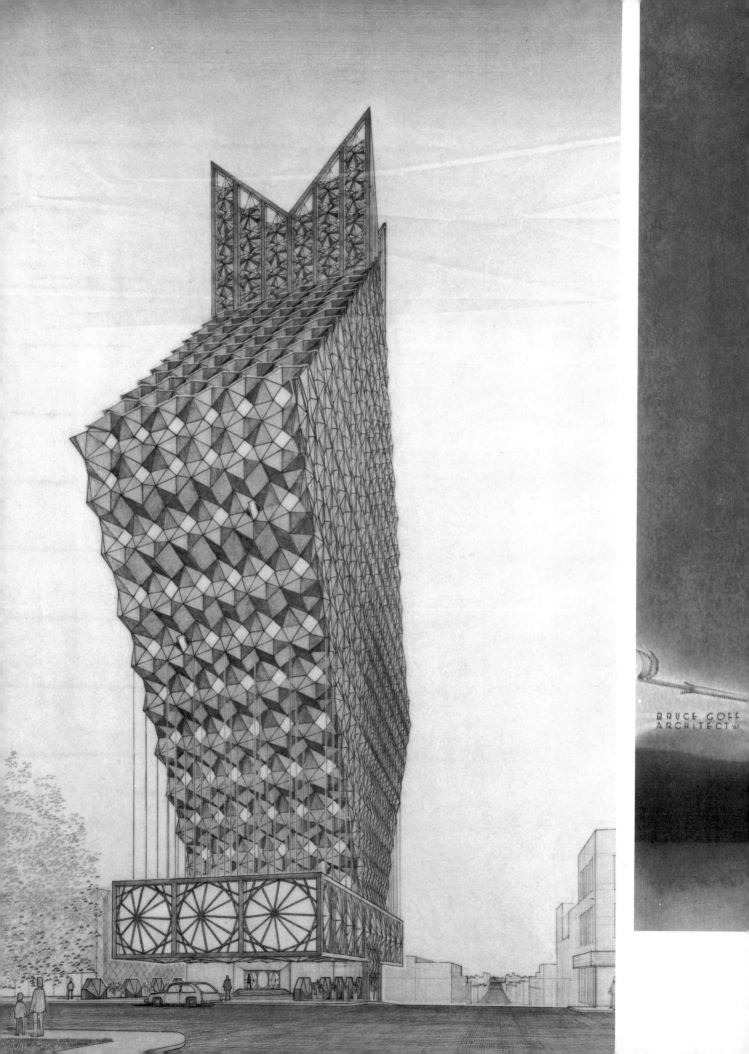

BRUCE GOFF
ARCHITECT '61

VIVA HOTEL   LAS VEGAS, NEVADA, U.S.A.

Bruce Alonzo Goff American, 1904-1982, Left: First National Bank, Independence, MO: Perspective, delineated by Larry W. Grantham, pencil on tracing paper with ink lettering, 1977, Gift of Shin'enKan, Inc. 1990.871.2 (Courtesy of The Art Institute of Chicago) Above: Viva Casino and Hotel: Perspective view, graphite on tracing paper, 1961, Gift of Shin'enKan, Inc.,1990.807.1 (Courtesy of The Art Institute of Chicago)

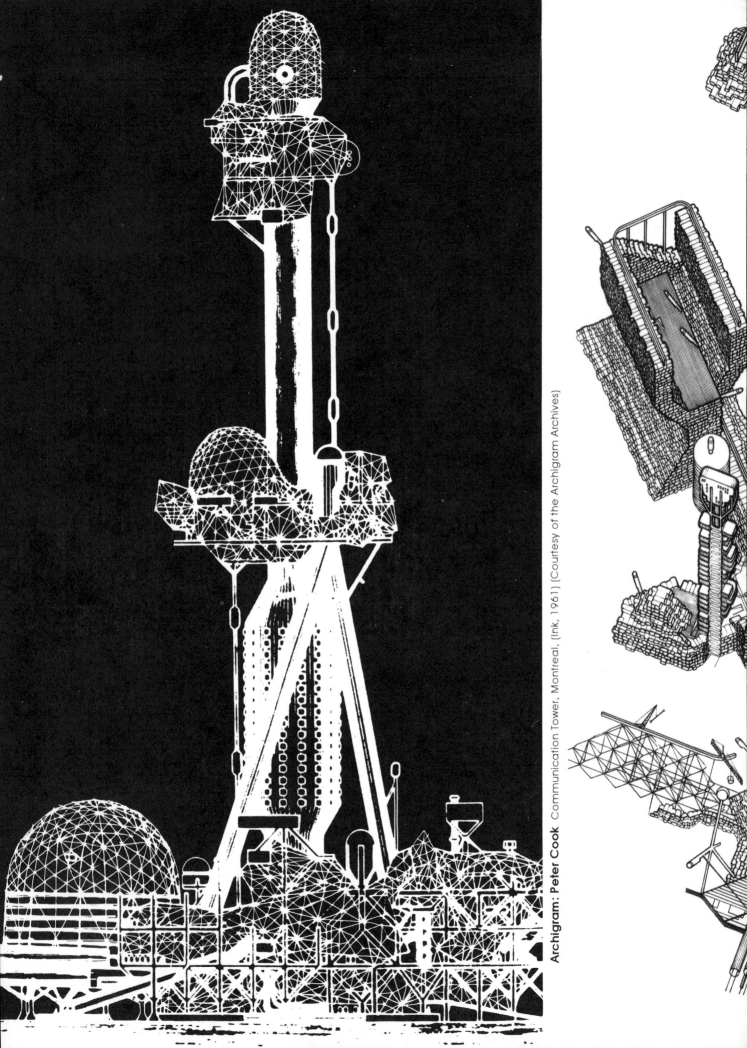

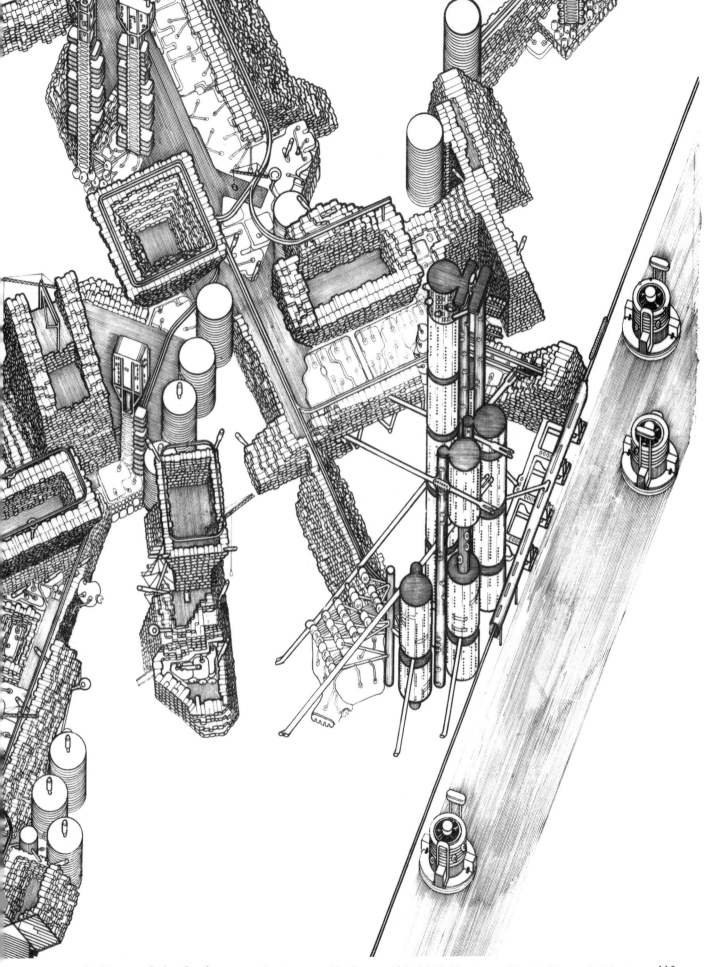

Archigram: Peter Cook Plug-In City: Axonometric (Pen and ink, 1964) (Courtesy of the Archigram Archives)   113

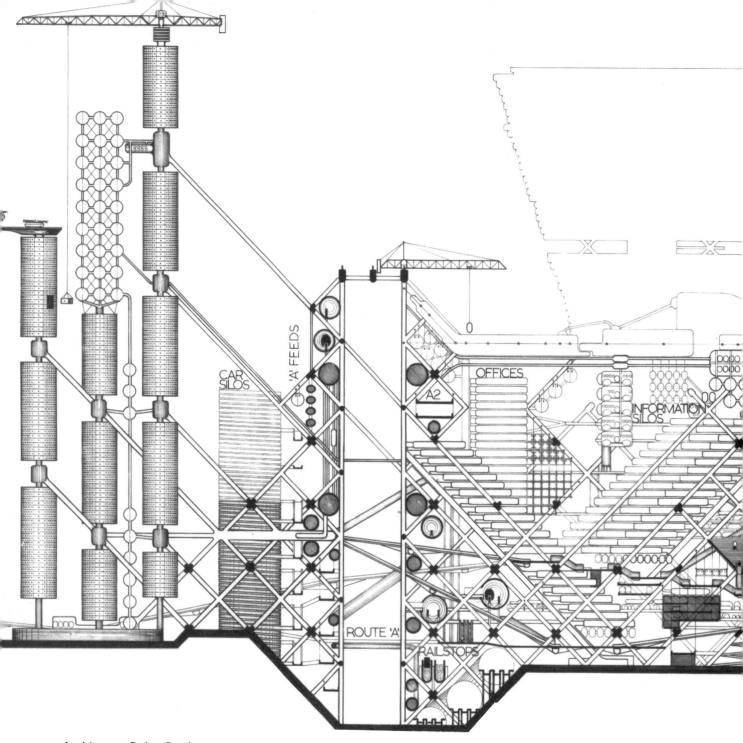

Archigram: Peter Cook Plug-In City: Longitudinal Section (Pen and ink, 1964)

114

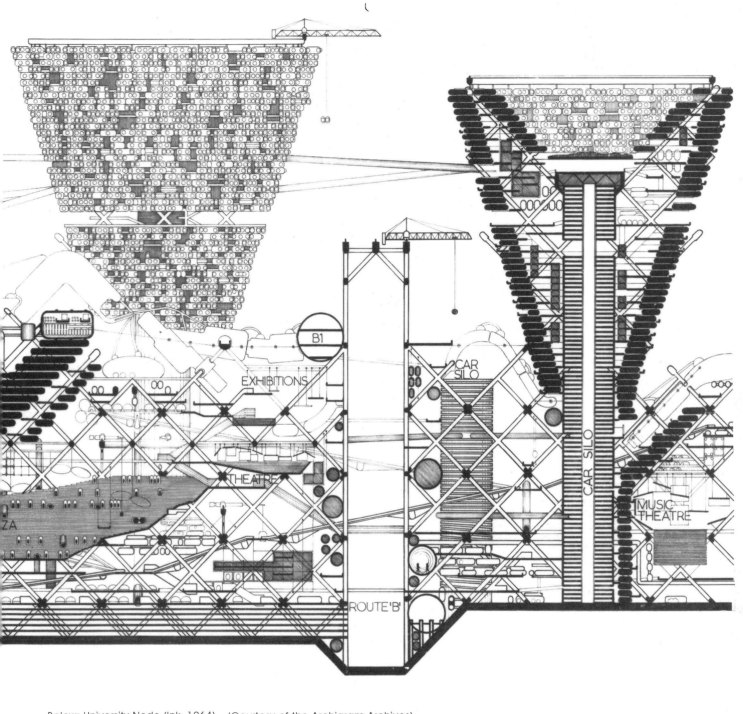

Below: University Node (Ink, 1964)   (Courtesy of the Archigram Archives)

Archigram: Ron Herron Walking Cities: Invading New York (Ink, photo-montage, 1964)   (Courtesy of the Archigram Archives)

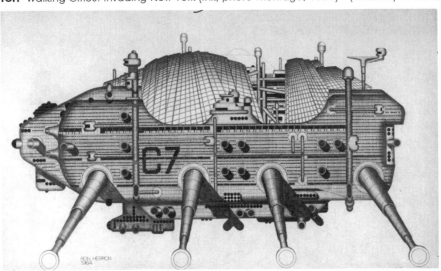

Walking Cities: Elevation (Ink, 1964)

Below: Walking Cities In the Desert (Colored Ink, airbrush, photo-montage, 1964)

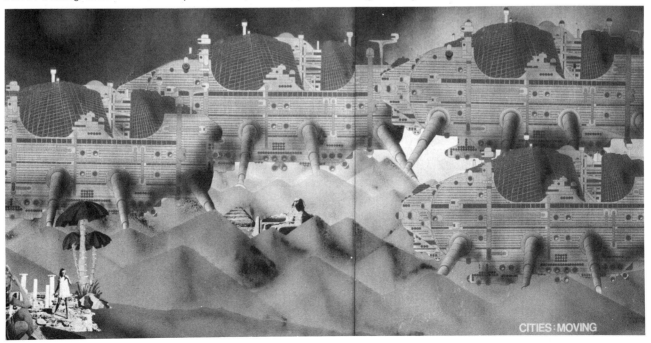

CITIES : MOVING

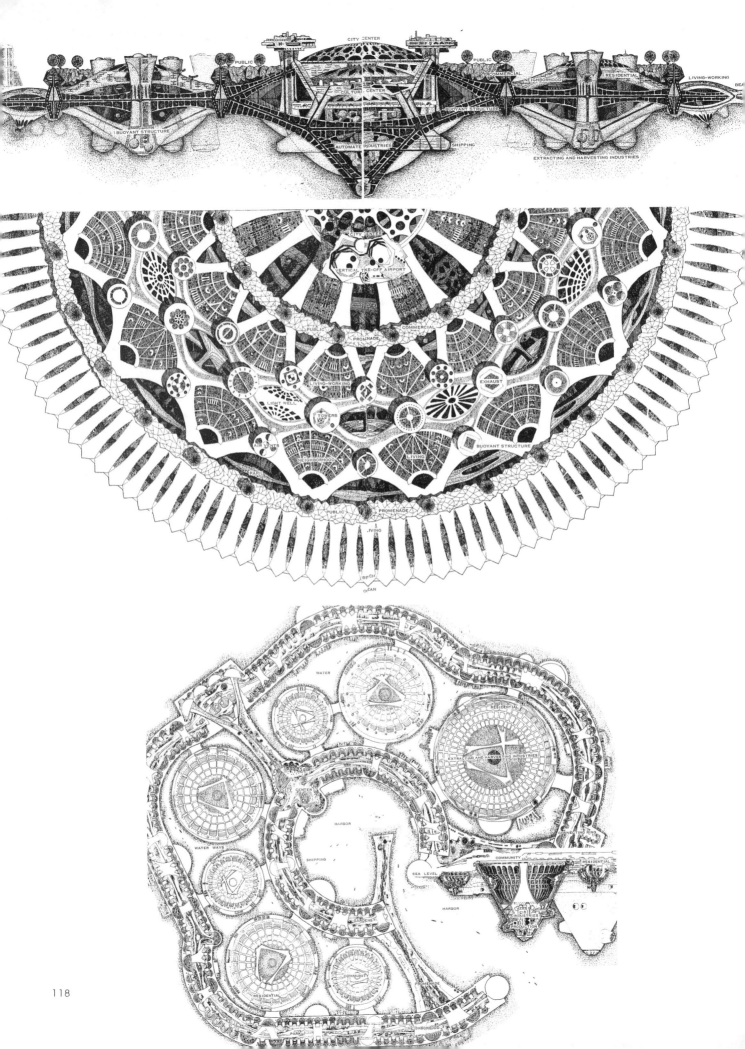

118

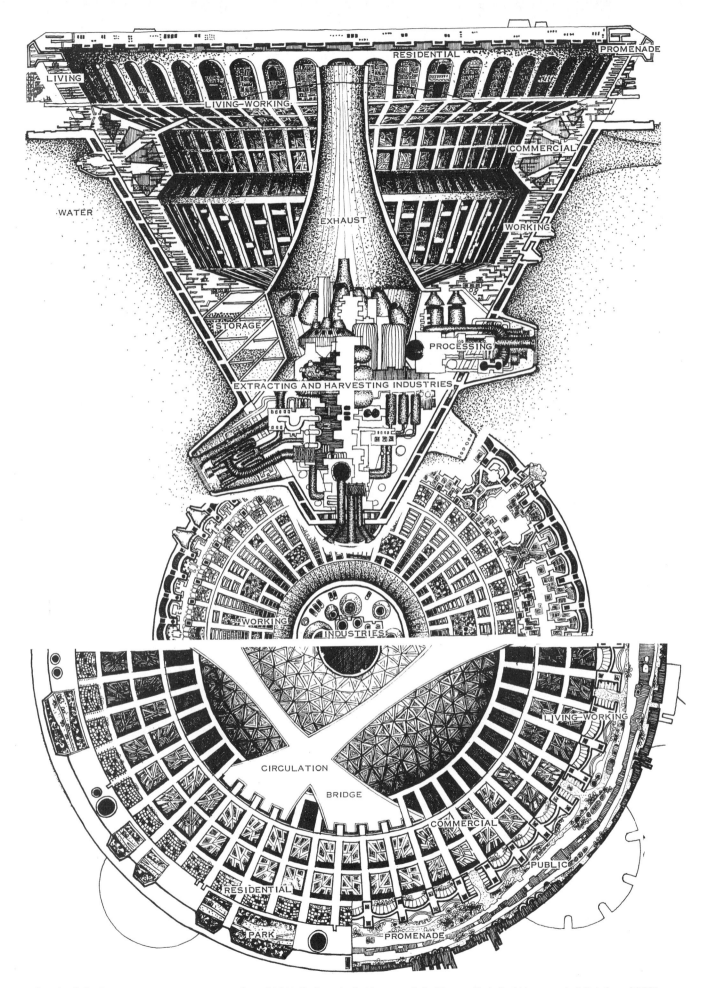

Paolo Soleri Top Left: Novanoah I (Ink line, 1969) Bottom Left: Novanoah II, Above: Detail of Novanoah II (Ink line, 1969)

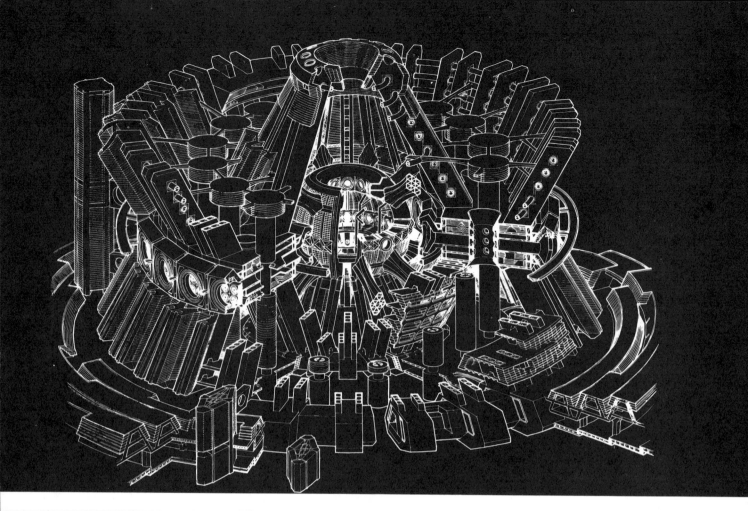

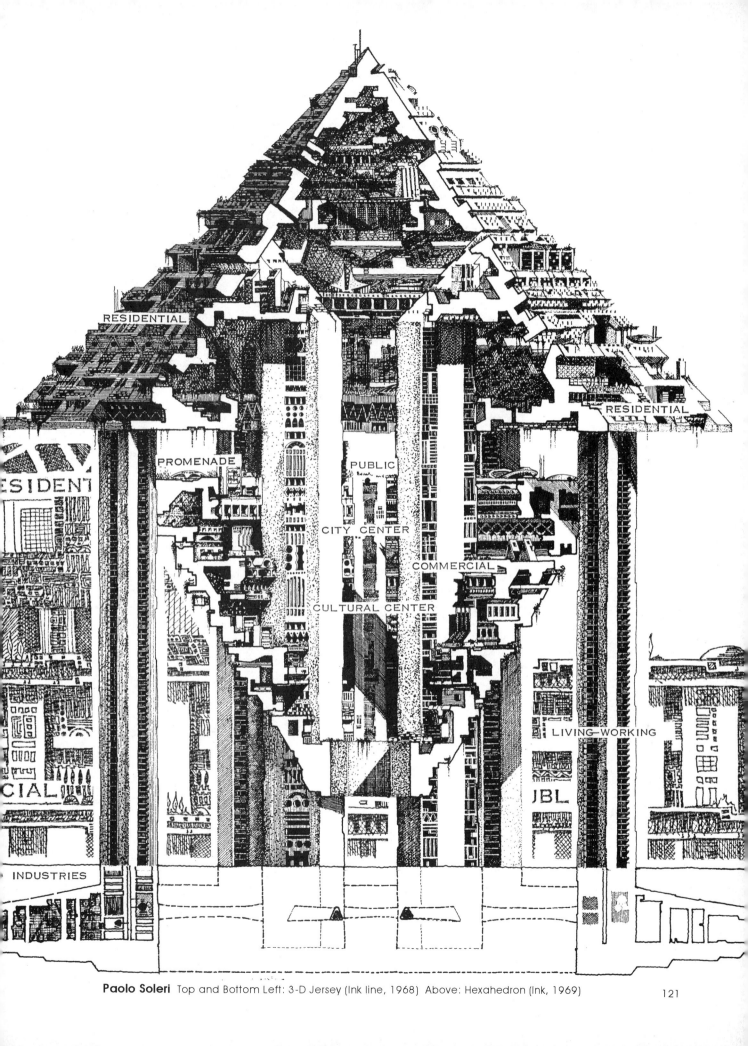

RESIDENTIAL

RESIDENTIAL

ESIDENT

PROMENADE

PUBLIC

CITY CENTER

COMMERCIAL

CULTURAL CENTER

CIAL

LIVING-WORKING

JBL

INDUSTRIES

Paolo Soleri Top and Bottom Left: 3-D Jersey (Ink line, 1968) Above: Hexahedron (Ink, 1969)

Herb Greene Exhibition Hall / Civic Arena (Ink on board, 1980)

Eugene Ray Bottom Left: Everett Solar Heated Villa, Lyons Valley, California (Colored pencil, 1982)
Bottom Right: Freeman Solar Heated Villa, Morro Bay, California (Colored pencil, 1980)

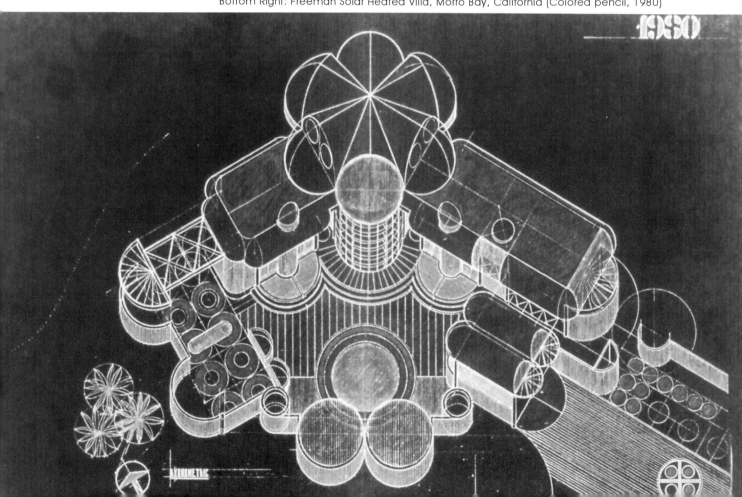

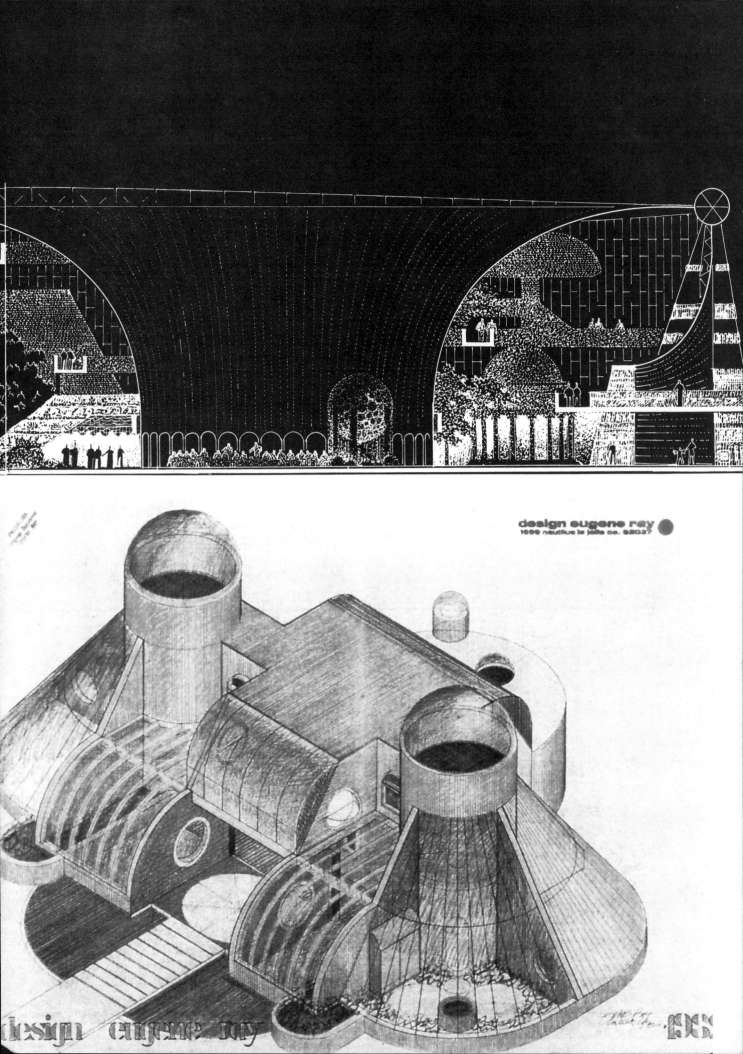

design eugene ray
1699 nautilus la jolla ca. 92037

design eugene ray 1968

Jacques Gillet Sketches of a Tomb for "My Friend Bruce Goff" (Colored pencil, 1983)   Left: Sculpture-Architecture along the Gorges Du Tarn, France, (Pencil, 1971)

Arthur Dyson Top Left: Michael Residence, Berkeley California (Ink on tracing paper, 1977)
Top Right: Millerton Residence, Madera County California (Pencil on vellum, 1984)
Bottom: Effie Office building, Fresno, California (Pencil on colored board, 1984)

Arthur Dyson Carlson Residence, Van Nuys, California (Airbrush and colored pencil, 1981)

Syd Mead Top: Golf Course Clubhouse. Bottom: Tokyo Night Club; Space Club (Opaque tempera, 1958)

Syd Mead Top: Minolta Marina. Bottom: Affrox; Linear City (Opaque tempera, 1958)

Stanley Tigerman Top: New York City (Ink line and colored pencil, 1983). Bottom: Lakeside (Ink line and colored pencil, 1983)

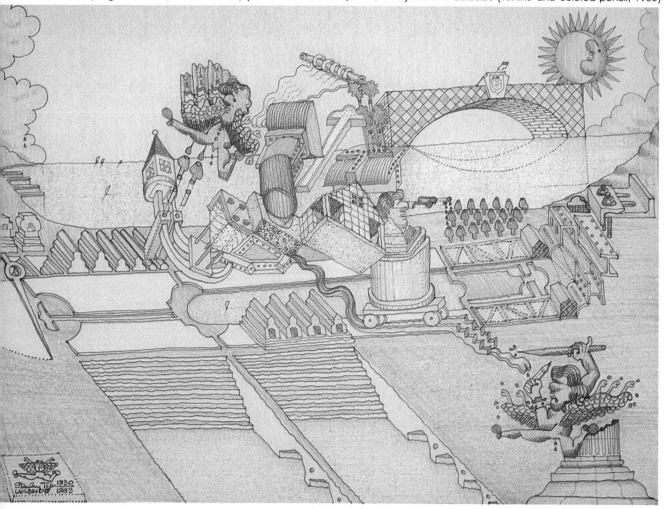

Stanley Tigerman Top: Career Collage (Ink line, colored pencil, 1983) Bottom: Myrtle Beach (Ink line, colored pencil, 1988)

"TORREVISTA"
THE HOME OF EUGENE TSUI AND FAMILY SCALE: 3/16" = ONE FOOT
TEJERAS, NEW MEXICO, U.S.A.
EUGENE TSUI, ARCHITECT BERKELEY, CALIFORNIA, U.S.A. JULY 25, 1986

"SOLARRIVE"
PASSIVE SOLAR RESEARCH CENTER FOR THE ARCTIC GAS PIPELINE COMPANY
NEAR FAIRBANKS, ALASKA JANUARY 9, 1987
EUGENE TSUI, ARCHITECT BERKELEY, CALIFORNIA
SCALE: APPROXIAMETLY 1/16 INCH EQUALS ONE FOOT

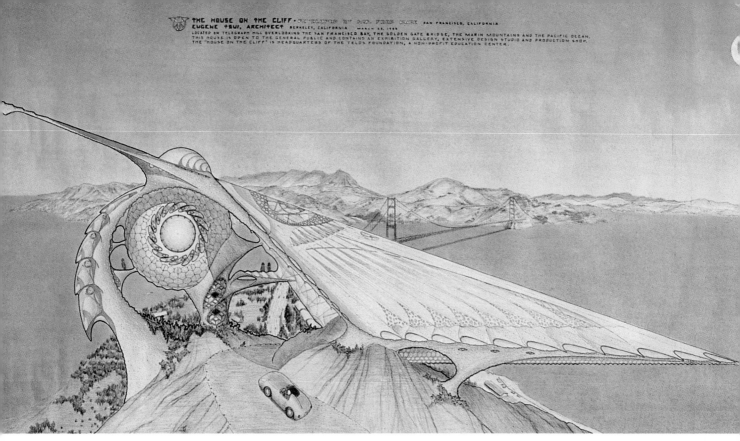

Eugene Tsui Top left: Torrevista, Studio of Eugene Tsui, Tejiras, New Mexico (Ink and colored pencil, 1988)
Bottom left: Solarrius; Passive Solar Energy Center for the Arctic Pipeline Company (Ink and colored pencil, 1987)
Above: House on a Cliff, San Francisco (Ink and colored pencil, 1988)
Below: Prototype Ravine Windmill Dwelling, Orinda, California (Ink and colored pencil, 1987)

OFFICE · APARTMENT · RESEARCH TOWER FOR THE
APPLE COMPUTER CORPORATION SCALE: 1/16" EQUALS 5 FEET
NEAR SAN JOSE, CALIFORNIA FEBRUARY 7, 1987
EUGENE TSUI, ARCHITECT BERKELEY, CALIFORNIA, U.S.A.

Eugene Tsui Office/Apartment/Research Tower for the Apple Computer Corporation (Ink and colored pencil, 1987)

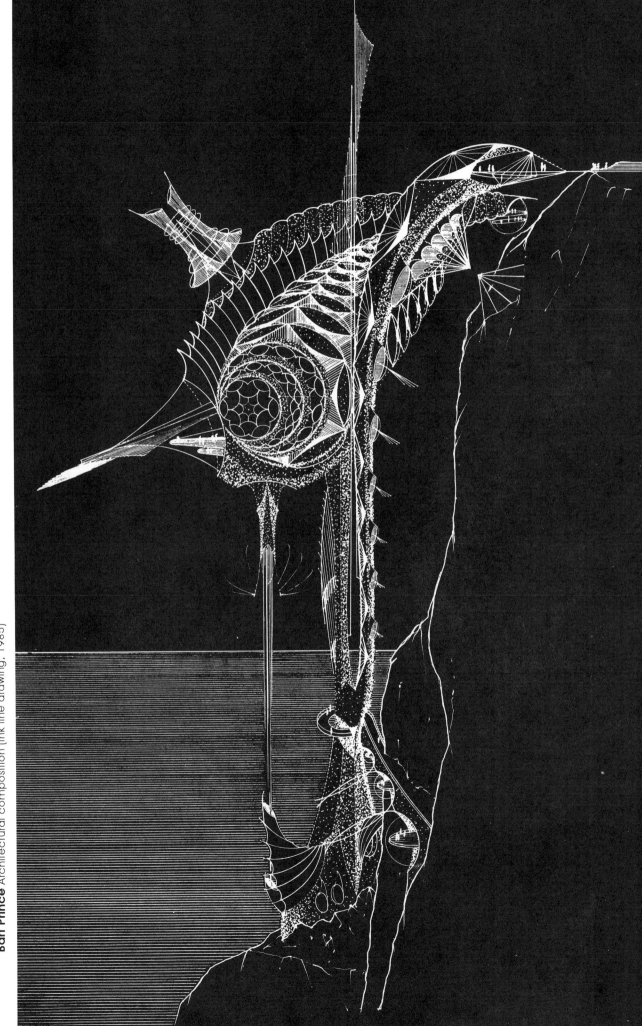

Bart Prince Architectural composition (Ink line drawing, 1985)

Davis Bite Study in Mass for a Cathedral (Pen and ink on board, 1965)

Gordon Baldwin Architectural studies (Ink, 1970)   **Bart Prince** Below: Indian Arts Center, Taos, New Mexico (Ink, 1985)

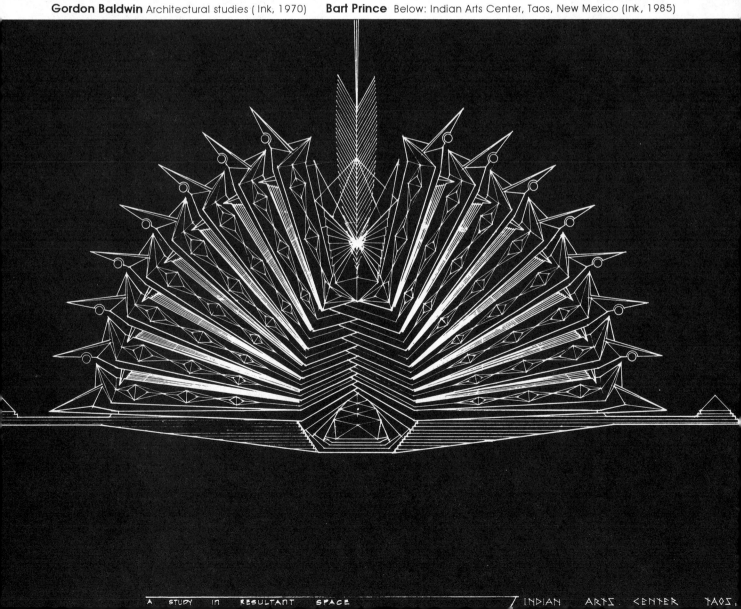

A STUDY IN RESULTANT SPACE   INDIAN ARTS CENTER TAOS,

Donald MacDonald Above: Pile House for San Francisco Bay (Colored pencil, 1987)
Bart Prince Opposite: Hanna House, Albuquerque, New Mexico (Ink, 1985)

Douglas Cooper Above: The Approach (Carbon pencil on paper, 1979) Collection of the artist
Left: Section Through Termite Mounds and Cupolas (Carbon pencil on paper, 1983)

141

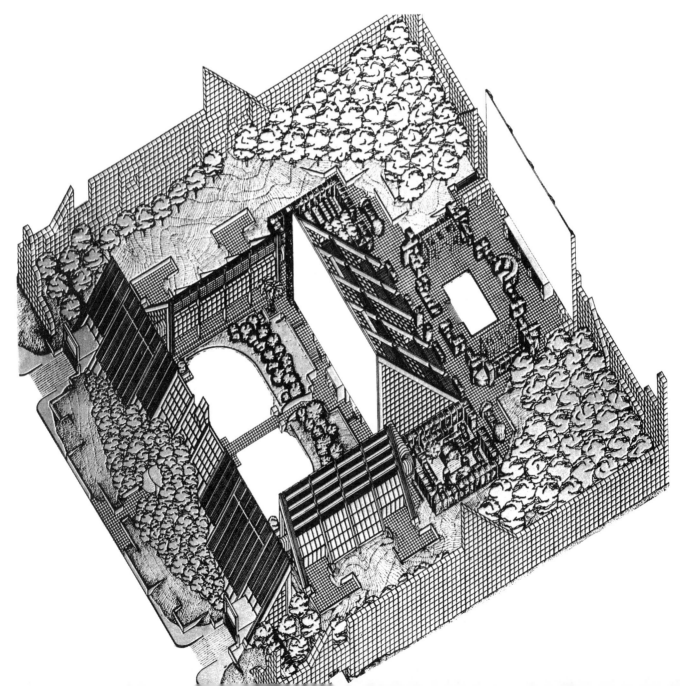

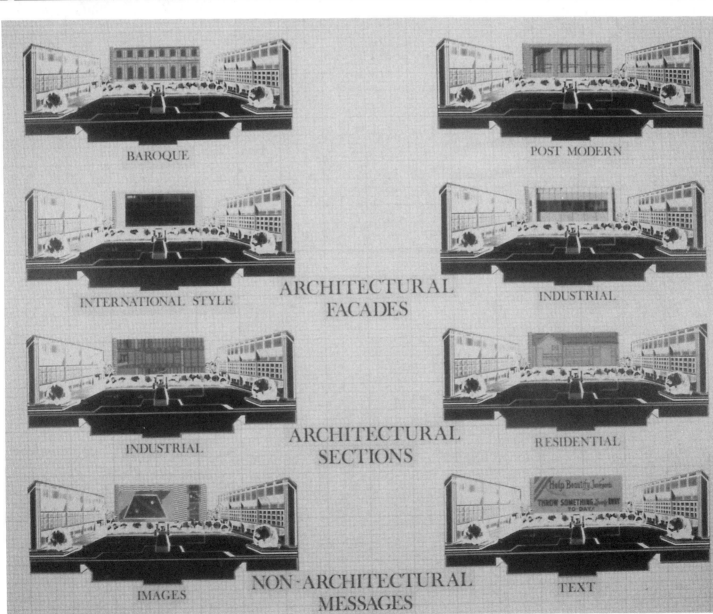

Hans Christian Lischewski Media House for Karl Friedrich Schinkel (Computer images, 1983)

Orest Places for People in the Year 2010: Terrestrial (Tempera on illustration board, 1985)

Orest Places for People in the Year 2010: Extraterrestrial (Tempera on illustration board, 1985)   145

Harvey Ferraro Above: Cloud Seeders/Wind Diverters/Worker's Settlement. (Ink, airbrush on illustration board, 1989)
Opposite: Test Tubes-R-Us: (Wax pencil, pastel on colored paper, 1985)

147

148   **Harvey Ferraro / Gretchen Marick** Movie Set Design (Pastel on tracing paper, 1987)

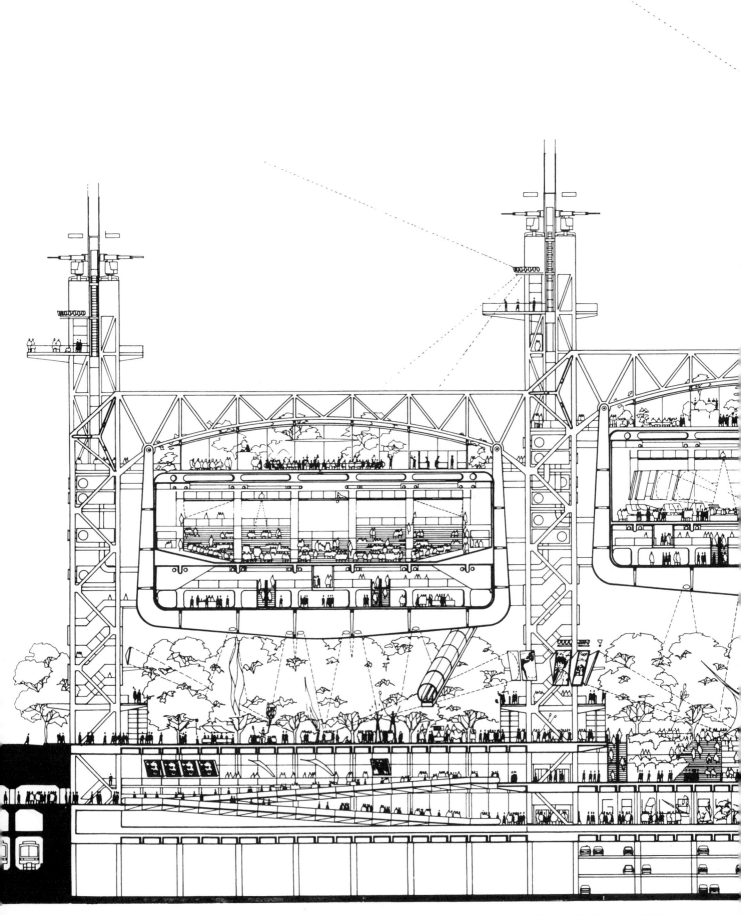

Richard Rogers Partnership Tokyo International Forum (1989) Design Competition Entry (Ink line, 1989)

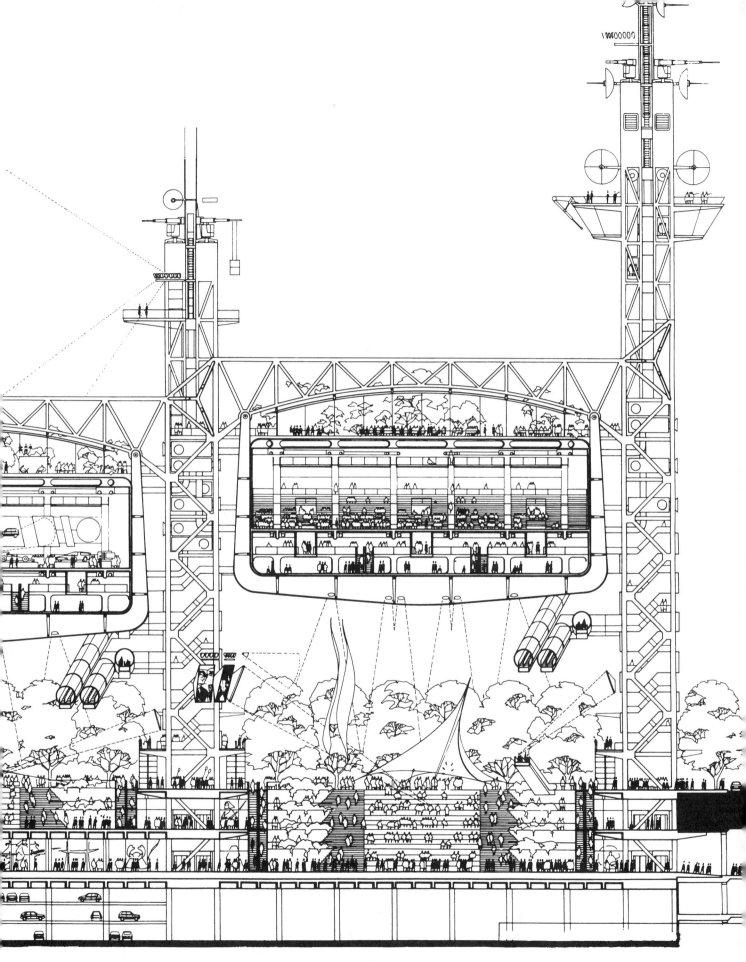

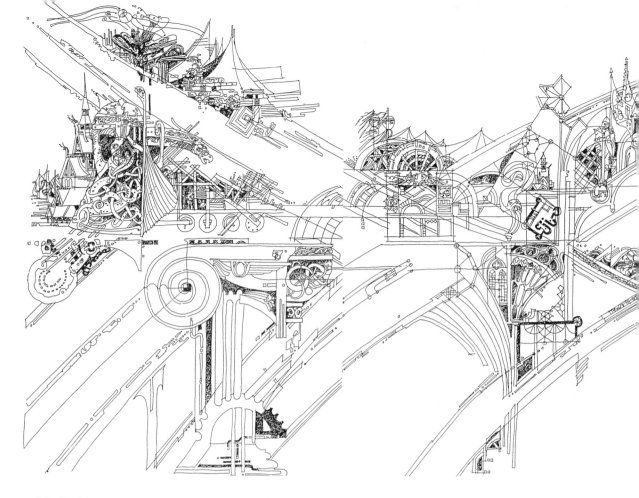

Martin Myers Above and Below: Wall Mural with architectural theme (Ink outline, 1989)

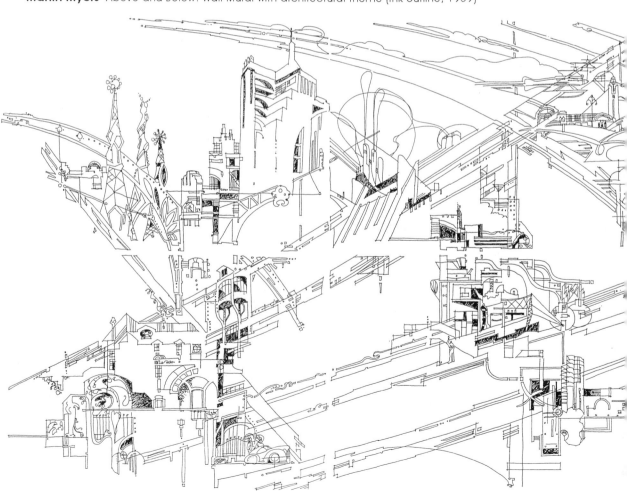

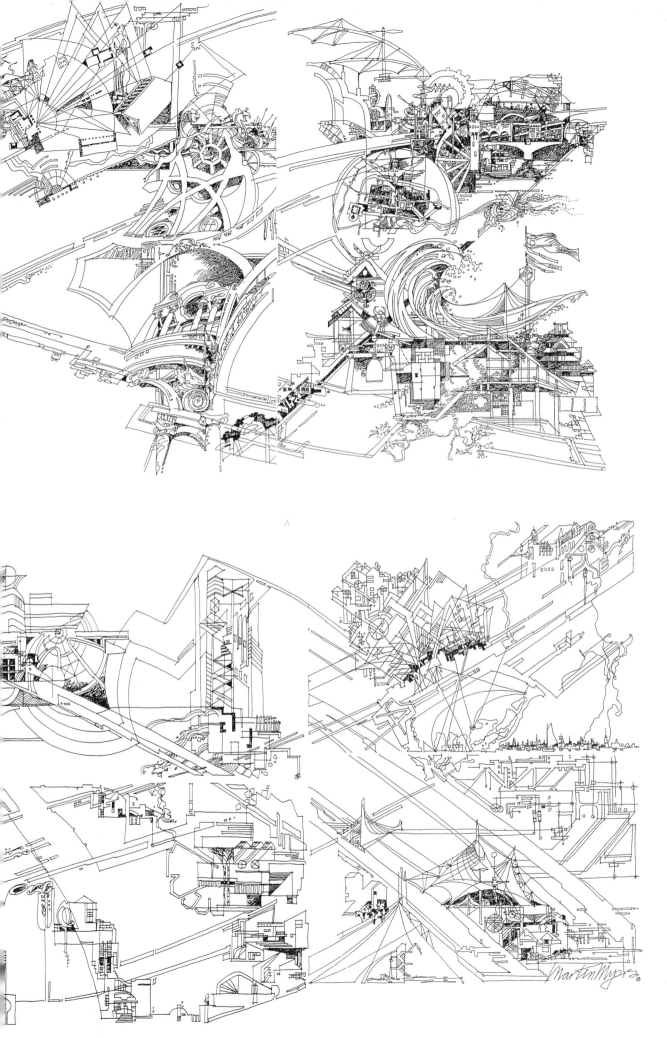

153

Albert Lorenz Above: The Renaissance in New York (Ink line and colored ink, 1989)
Below: The United States (Ink, 1989)

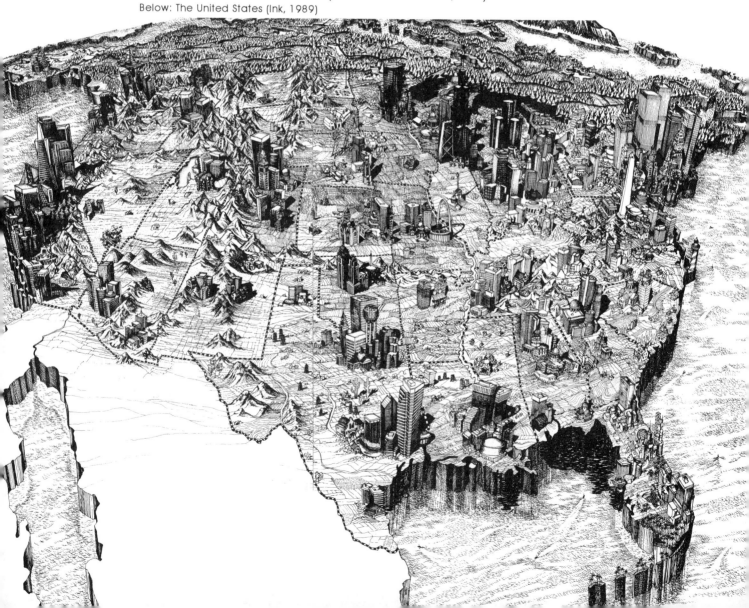

Gordon Grice Fixing our Future (Ink on mylar, 1996) (Color pencil over ink line original, 1997)

Lee Dunnette Astronaut's Memorial (Pastel on illustration board, 1989)

156

Arthur Cotton Moore Top: Decorative Rooftop Exhaust Fans (1989)   Bottom: Asymmetrical Pipe Capital with Industrial Light Fixture (1989)

(Acrylic, ink on canvas and colored pencil on paper, 1989)

Lebbeus Woods City of Air (Pencil, 1981)

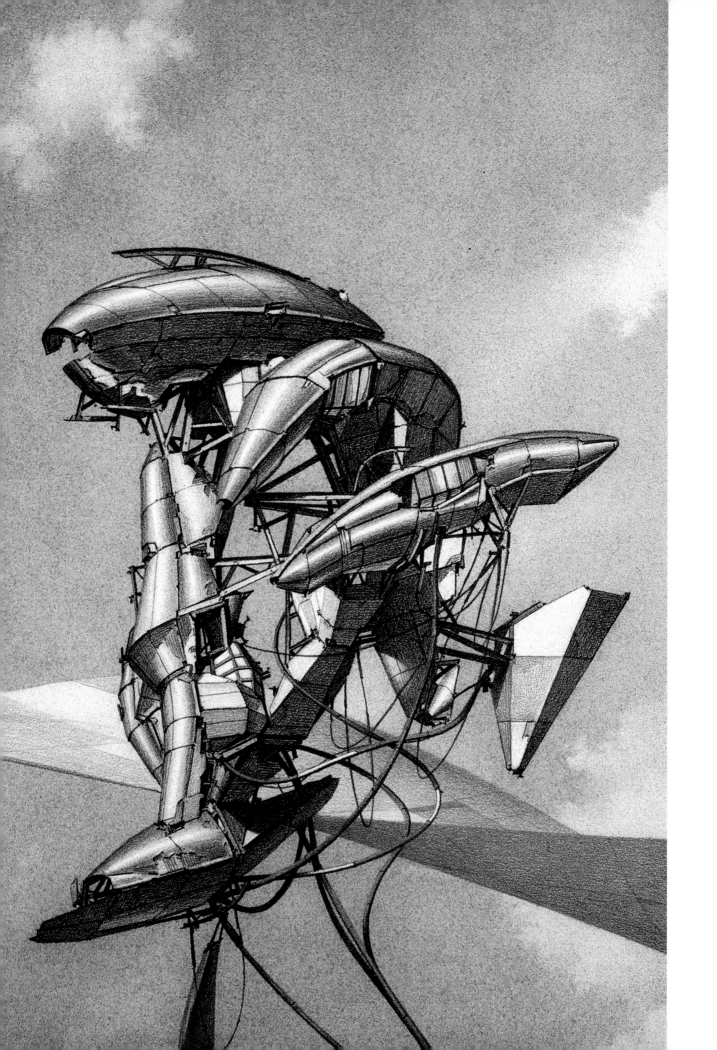

Lebbeus Woods Left: Aerial Paris (Ink line and colored pencil, 1993)
Above: War and Architecture (Ink line and colored pencil, 1993)
Below: War and Architecture (Ink line and colored pencil, 1993)

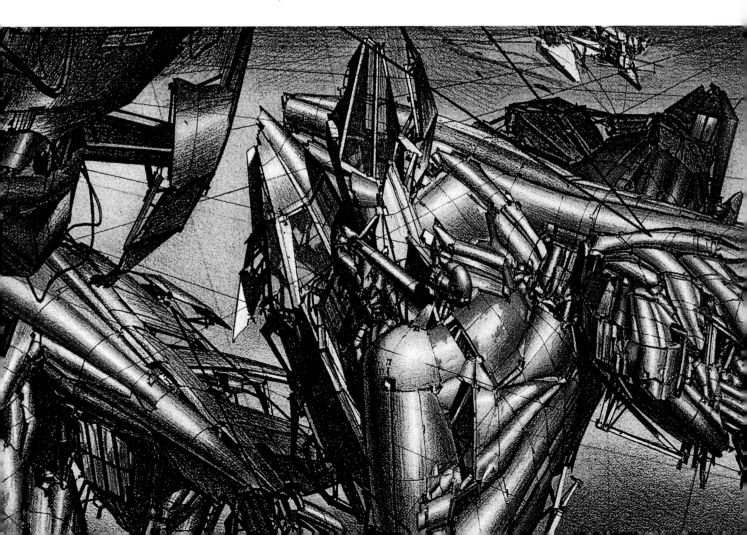

Gilbert Gorsky *Demeter and Dionysus* (Colored pencil, 1989)

Gilbert Gorski   Above: Random Access Memory (Etching, 1998)
Opposite: Demeter and Dionysus (Colored pencil, 1989)

164

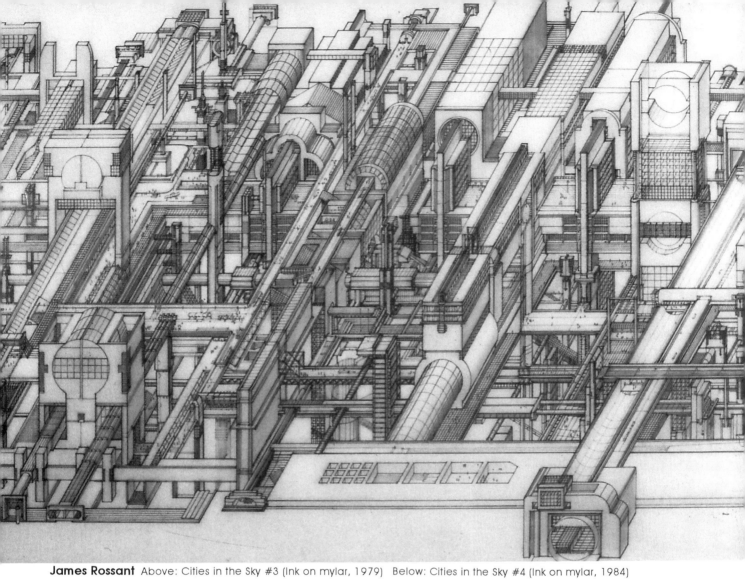

James Rossant Above: Cities in the Sky #3 (Ink on mylar, 1979)   Below: Cities in the Sky #4 (Ink on mylar, 1984)

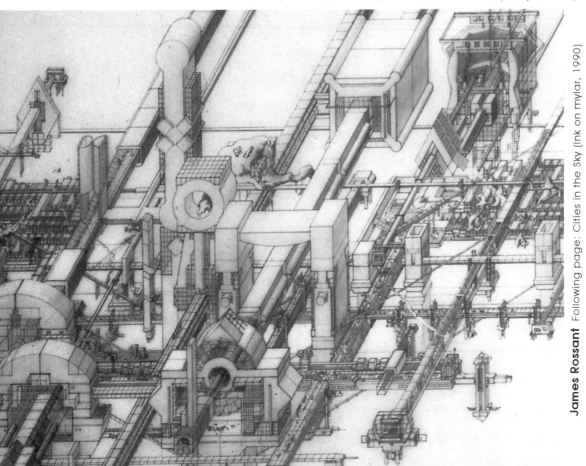

James Rossant Following page: Cities in the Sky (Ink on mylar, 1990)

165

The TOWER of Babel

Ian McKay Above: Babel- The Infinite City: #1 (Ink on paper, 1996)
Albert Lorenz Opposite: The Tower of Babel (Ink, 1990)

Ian McKay Babel- The Infinite City: #2 (Ink on paper, 1996)　Opposite: Babel- The Infinite City: #3 (Ink, 1996)

Frank M. Costantino Hancock Axial 1 (Watercolor, 1995)

Jeffrey Michael George *New De Anza Hotel (Watercolor and tempera on board, 1990)*

Orest Above: San Francisco Mixed Use Project (Tempera on illustration board, 1989)
Opposite: New York City Waterfront Competition (Tempera on illustration board, 1989)

Nancy Wolf Top: Lost City (Pencil on paper, 1988) (Collection: Linda Joy Goldner and Robert J. Segal)
Bottom: Billboard Dreams (Carbon pencil on paper, 1989)
Opposite: New Realities (Pencil on paper, 1990) (Collection Robert S. Perry)

Nancy Wolf

Top: Pilgrimage (Acrylic on canvas, 1993) Collection: Robert S. Perry.
Bottom Left: Hall of Vanities (Acrylic on canvas, 1989)
Collection Robert S. Perry
Bottom Right: Ideal City (Colored pencil and collage, 1987)
Collection: James and Marsha Matevka

179

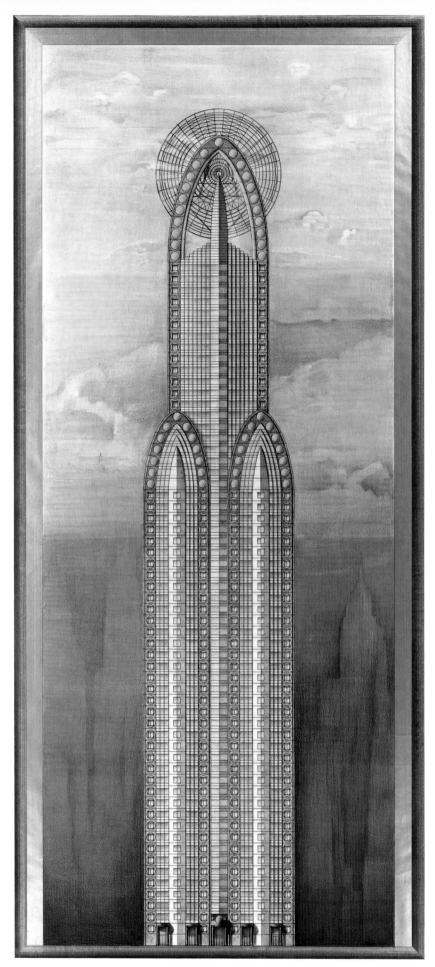

Tad Berezowski

Left: Imaginary Tower (Colored pencil on vellum, 1990)
Above: Tower (Colored pencil on vellum, 1990)
Right: Villa (Colored pencil on vellum, 1990)

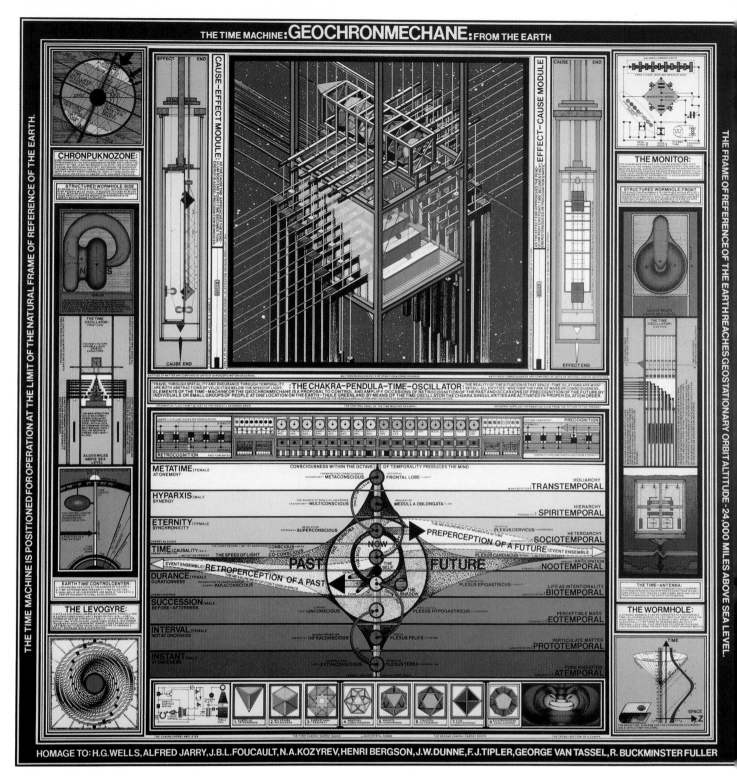

Paul Laffoly GEOCHRONMECHANE: The Time Machine From Earth (Oil, acrylic, lettering and ink on primed canvas, 1993)

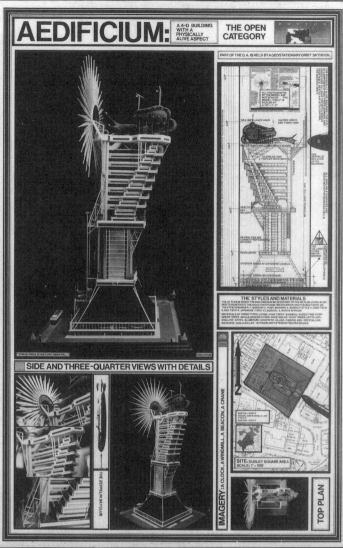

Paul Laffoly Quartum Dimensio Aedificium, (Ink, photo-collage and letters on board, 1987)
Urpflanze Haus, (Ink, 1993)

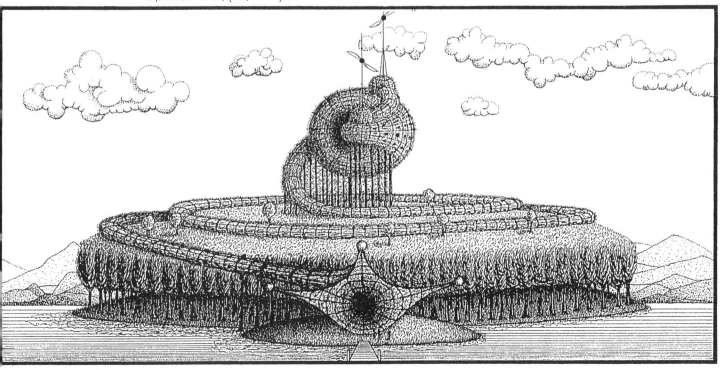

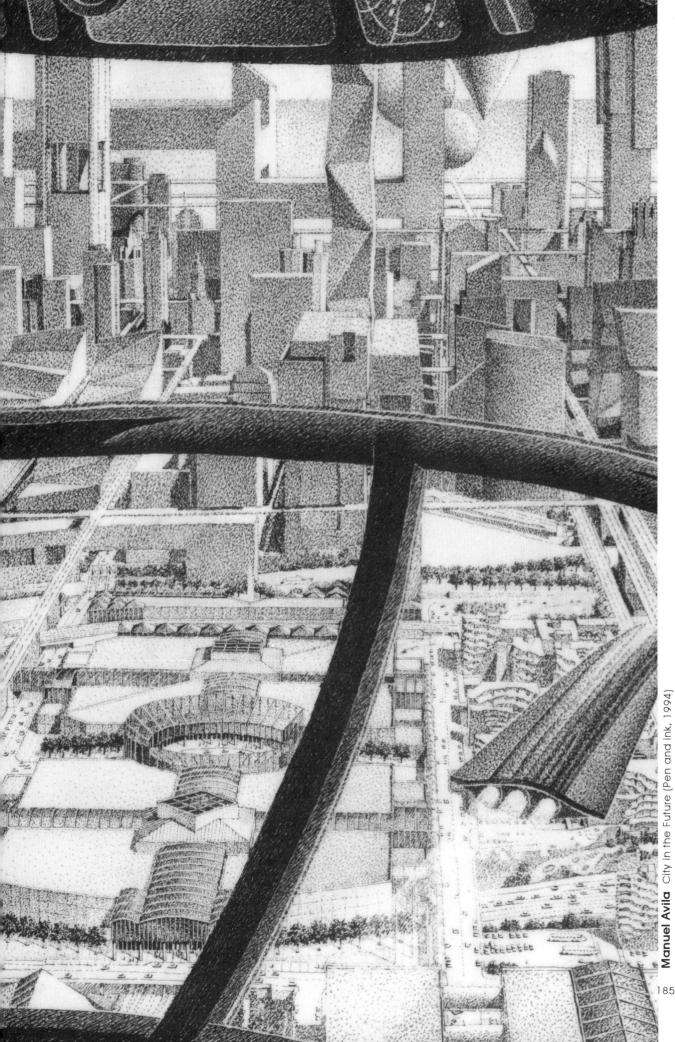

Manuel Avila City in the Future (Pen and ink, 1994)

Ernest Burden III Organic bridge (Pencil on board, 1994)

187

Kevin Woest Bridge Habitat: Detail of tower and overall view (Ink line on paper, 1995)

Richard Ferrier Above: Windows and Fragments; Memory and Desire (Watercolor, graphite, metallic paint, and photographic images, 1994)
Below: Detail from Ousley Watercolor (Watercolor, 1998)

Ron Love Edge City; Experimentation with Architectural Form (1995)

Robert McIlhargey Left: Space Park, Breman, Germany (Colored ink and pencil, 1997)
Robert McIlhargey / Lori Brown Above and Below: New World Entertainment Complex, Hawaii (Colored ink, airbrush, 1997)

Christopher Grubbs Entrance to Ikpiari, Tokyo, Japan (Colored pencil on board, 1997)

David Joiner Galaxeum: Proposed Space Museum, Observatory and Planetarium (Watercolor and guache, 1995)   195

196 **Sergei Tchoban** Monument (Watercolor, pen and ink, 1994)

Sergei Tchoban Spaces for an Art Exhibition. (Watercolor, pen and sepia ink, 1995)

198

James Akers Battersea Power Station Development Project, London (Pencil, 1995)

199

Thomas W. Schaller Orpheus in Orlando (Watercolor, 1995)

Fernando Torre-Sarlet Columbus Circle Office/Residential/Retail Complex (Pencil, colored markers, 1995)
James Parakh Opposite: Office Towers above Penn Station (Ink line drawing, 1990)

James Akers Tech Tower-2.4M (Watercolor and pencil, 1998) **James Parakh** Opposite: Toronto Skymall (Ink, 1990)

Lius Roidan Chapel in Concrete and Glass (Penci, 1995) (Courtesy, San Francisco Institute of Architecture)

Lius Roidan Ski Lodge Co-op (Pencil, 1995) (Courtesy, San Francisco Institute of Architecture)

Yves Rathle

Left: Bagna mixed-use tower, Bankok, Thailand (Ink and colored markers, 1997)
Above and Below: HMV/Rock and Roll Hall of Fame
Prototype Theme Store (Ink and colored markers, 1997)

Imre Makovecz Above: Sketch of Tower: Lutheran Church, Siofok (Pencil, 1986)
Below: Sketch, Church of Kolozsvar (Cluj – Romania) (Pencil, 1995)

Imre Makovecz The Bartok Performances: Stage Set Construction (Pencil, 1993)

Sadaka Kinuta Above: Concerto (Acrylic, airbrush, colored pencil on watercolor paper, 1997)
Stephan Hoffpauir Below: Sony Station: Virtual Theme Park. (Watercolor and pastel, 1998)

Hans Christian Lischewski *Cybercities, (Computer Images, 1997)*

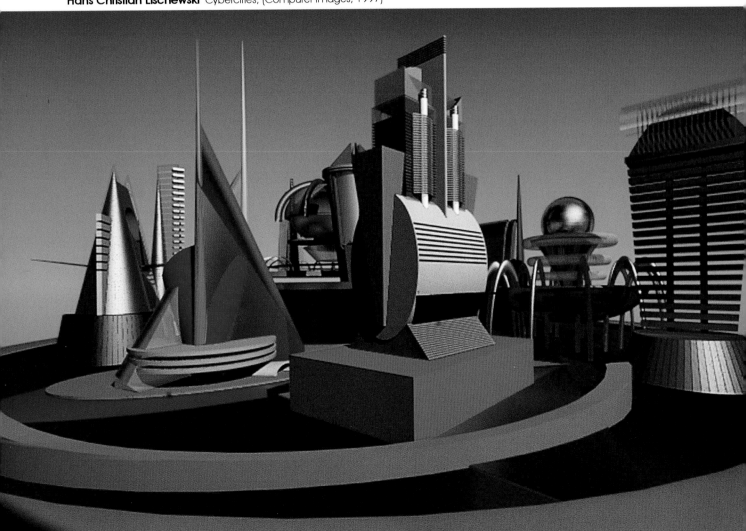

Batman Forever Concept sketches for scenery and backgrounds for the Warner Bros. Film. Courtesy of Photofest, New York City

The Fifth Element Computer rendering by Digital Domain. Courtesy of Photofest, New York City

STAR WARS, Episode One: The Phantom Menace. Still image from the film Courtesy of Photofest, New York City

BLADERUNNER Above: Still image, street scene from the film (Courtesy of Photofest, New York City)

THE FIFTH ELEMENT Still image from Columbia Pictures's science fiction film. (Courtesy of Photofest, New York City)

Ernest Burden III Exile: From a Prison's Portfolio, after Piranesi's Il Carceri (Pencil on paper, 1999)

WHAT DREAMS MAY COME Still image from the film (1999) (Courtesy of Photofest, New York City)

NOTES On The Plates

2-3 Giovanni Battista Piranesi Architectural Sketch done for Robert Adam.

Piranesi also influenced an entire generation of creative, Neoclassical architects who came to Rome to study its lessons. Robert Adam, Piranesi's favorite and most famous student, was impressed by his master's intensity. This can be seen in his improvisations on classical themes and the impromptu fantasy drawing he made for Adam.

4-5 Giovanni Battista Piranesi Architectural Sketch.

In this sketch Piranesi's pen does not let the architectural images stand still; they hover with a point and counterpoint. The architectural forms express the force of nature, swirling in space. His virtuoso draughtsmanship relies as much upon the transformative powers of art as upon archaeological evidence to persuade his readers of the glory that was Rome.

6-7 Giovanni Battista Piranesi Architectural Fantasy.

Piranesi's vision of Rome was not nostalgic but Utopian. He realized that if ancient Rome could not be brought back to life materially, its spirit could be invoked to inspire future generations. For him, the monuments of Rome became a potent metaphor for modernity. The chiaroscuro character of the 18th century - the order and excess – inspired the architect Giambattista Piranesi (1720 - 78) to express his visions of an urban environment.

His images always originated in historical fact, yet they soon veered into imaginative fantasy. This mixture of artifice and archaeology forms a constant element of Piranesi's style. It originates, at least in part, in his early training in stage design in his native Venice. There he mastered the technique of the *scena per angolo*, a radical concept developed by the Bibiena family of theatrical designers. Here, the traditional single-point perspective was replaced by a series of diagonal axes which cut across the stage, opening up a succession of vistas and offering unlimited potential for depicting architectural space.

In his etchings, Piranesi applied the exaggerated perspectives of the *scena per angolo* to the city of Rome, draping the images in dramatic shafts of light which transformed the city into a stage so viewers could explore each nook of these ancient ruins with their eyes.

8-9 Giuseppe Galli Bibiena Theatrical Stage Design.

The Bibiena family, who, under eight names, created theatrical designs in a style so consistent that their whole work looks as though it might have been done by one man at one time. Guiseppe was the inheritor and brilliant exploiter of the family's skills and inventions. The Baroque was the supreme age of illusion, and at their drawing boards, unhampered by the need for permanence, summed up the great emotional architecture of the Baroque.

10-11 Giovanni Battista Piranesi The Prisons, Plate XIII.

The *Carceri* show the shadow side of urbanity. Although littered with instruments of torture, these scenes do not depict sadistic punishment but rather they conceive of architectural space itself as a prison. The phantom dwellers of the *Carceri* are not so much incarcerated as overwhelmed by the superhuman scale of their surroundings. Piranesi's architectural hyperboles

become semi-abstract studies in which order and anarchy coexist. In their evocation of man-made structures sprawling out of control, the *Carceri* seem to prefigure Modern images of the mechanized city, immortalized in Expressionist films such as *Metropolis.*

12-13 Joseph Michael Gandy Sir John Soane's Public and Private Buildings.

This hypothetical collection of images depicting the work of Europe's most revered architect, Sir John Soane, was a tribute to Soane's genius, as well as Gandy's talent. The buildings appear either as models, or as framed paintings, as if sitting around an attic or storeroom. The unusual effect of lighting dramatizes the scene, allowing contrasts and using shadows to add a sense of realism to the unusual composite.

14-15 Thomas Cole The Course of Empire: The Consumption of Empire.

As one of a five-part allegorical series, this giant painting illustrates an idyllic setting with imagined architectural forms softened by drapery, reflections in the water, and the play of light and shadows.

16-17 Emmaneul Brune Principal Staircase of the Palace of a Sovereign.

The new Paris Opera House of Charles Garnier became the great influence after 186. By 1863, brightly colored and heavily decorated drawings appeared in the winning projects for the Grand Prix at the Ecole des Beaux-Arts. This staircase design is no exception. It directly adapts details of the Opera House, which was then still in the drawing stage.

18-19 Erastus Salisbury Field Historical Monument of the American Republic.

Towers in different architectural styles spring high in the air from a long base that almost fills the fourteen-foot width of the canvas. Every level of every tower is keyed to an incident in American history and illustrated as bas-relief or as sculpture. In the highest rooms Field envisioned exhibitions illustrating everyday life. His crowning imagery is the aerial railway with balloon-stack engines connecting the exhibition rooms of seven of the eight towers.

20-21 Louis-Hippolyte Boileau Casino

This festive design for a casino relies heavily on pictorial effects and suggests some of the preoccupation with Art Nouveau, particularly in its "Gaudiesque" grottoes.

22-23 Frank Lloyd Wright Wolf Lake Amusement Park.

The origins of the commission for this project remain unclear. It was an ambitious project at the beginning of Wright's career, as he had been practicing for just two years. The 1893 Columbia Exposition, in Wright's opinion was a great tragedy because it heralded Neoclassical forms as the style to imitate. This design shows a waterfront situation, such as existed at the Columbia Exposition, but Wright had enhanced the shore with buildings more inherently appropriate to the site.

24 Frank Lloyd Wright Lake Tahoe Summer Colony.

This was one of the first commissions to come to Wright's newly established Los Angeles office. It was for an inn with accompanying cabins, cottages, and barges at Emerald Bay on Lake Tahoe, California. The drawings were the first that Mr. Wright made using a new technique, employing colored pencils instead of his traditional watercolors. Although the project turned out to be a phony scheme by the real-estate corporation to sell lots using Wrights name, the designs and drawings produced for the project are among his best.

25 Frank Lloyd Wright Gordon Strong Planetarium.

This project was designed to attract the motor-touring craze, wherein people would visit the wilderness regions in their cars. It was called the Automotive Objective, and would be located on Sugarloaf Mountain, Maryland. The outside view reveals the landscape of the earth, while inside there was a planetarium. The main theme was the use of a spiral ramp connecting the various levels.

Although this project was never realized, the spiral concept came up in the Pittsburgh Point Park Civic Center, and again in the V,C. Morris Shop in San Francisco, and finally in the Guggenheim Museum in New York. It was here that the idea was born.

26-27 Frank Lloyd Wright Doheny Ranch Resort.

This project gave Wright the opportunity to show how a landscape could be respected by the architecture and preserved. On one drawing in the series he wrote: "The whole becomes a terraced garden suitable to the region". He later wrote an additional caption on this drawing, "An attempt to preserve the native beauty of the Hollywood hills by preserving all natural contours and growth – embroidering the hills with architecture, the road itself becoming architecture as a part of the houses themselves".

28 Raymond Hood Apartments on a Bridge. Rendering by Hugh Ferriss.

Architect Raymond Hood outlined the plausible possibility of utilizing the framework of bridges for apartments or offices. The idea could, of course, be visualized in various forms – in the accompanying sketch, the suspension type of bridge is assumed; the towers rise up into fifty or sixty story buildings; the serried structure being suspended – the buildings literally hung from cables.

At first glance it would appear that such a location for offices or residences is unusually desirable as to exposure, light and air. We may naturally assume landing stages, at the bases of the towers, for launch, yacht and hydroplane – whence it would be only a minute by elevator, to one's private door.

Facetious minds have suggested that the placing of apartments in such a fashion would introduce a bizarre – not to say dangerous – element into domestic life! On the other hand, serious minds have claimed that the project is not only sound but possesses unusual financial advantages.
Hugh Ferris, The Metropolis of Tomorrow, 1929.

29 Joseph D. Murphy Restaurant in the Air, Beaux Arts Competition.

This drawing received a prize in competition for the Beaux Arts Institute of Design. The problem was to develop a restaurant in a park with an elevation from which one could get a view of the surrounding landscape. The restaurant was to be on two levels, the lower of which was to be fifty feet above the ground. Murphy's design, done in pastels, reflects the influence of Frank Lloyd Wright in its massing, and an Art Deco influence in the detailing.

30-31 METROPOLIS Still scene from the movie.

Metropolis is one of the most expressive film testimonies of its age. It is a film of powerfully expressive archi-

tectural metaphors, a gallery of contemporary visions, and an important turning point in the development of film architecture.

Having had architectural training himself, Director Fritz Lang often intervened in the design process. Designing an architectural vision in film was a completely new challenge. They had never before conceived buildings that did not have relation to direct historic models. The director's efforts concentrated on the view into the city streets underneath the "New Tower of Babel." In the film, the memory of the biblical Tower of Babel is revived in a dream sequence obviously based on Pieter Bruegel's famous painting of 1563. They devoted much attention to the tower in the background, giving it a massive, threatening form.

Photos of canyon-like streets in New York City, where office employees never saw daylight, had been very popular in early architecture magazines. especially since World War I. The director introduced such streets on a scale that exceeded anything that existed in America at the time. In this film the architect had replaced the set designer.

For the impressive view into the street "canyon" an eighteen-foot-deep perspective model was built out of wood, plaster, canvas, and cardboard. The effect of motion was achieved by shooting frame by frame, and by individually advancing each car, airplane, train, and elevator between each shot. These techniques became the basics for animated sequences for the next fifty years.

32-33 JUST IMAGINE Still scene from the film.

In *Just Imagine*, probably the first science fiction musical ever, New York City is presented as it would look like fifty years in the future. The film depicts a completely changed skyline, nine levels of traffic, and private airplanes for everyone. It was filmed in 1929, when the celebrated architectural delineator Hugh Ferriss published his collected drawings of visionary skyscrapers, *Metropolis of Tomorrow*.

The film's sets make clear reference to Ferriss's compelling vision. Buildings gleam with electricity. Traces of earlier historic buildings are seen, their facades dissolved into rows and rows of brightly lit windows. It was clearly meant as a response to the success of *Metropolis*. The film aimed at surpassing its predecessor's design extravaganzas by erecting a vast miniature model of the city.

Films like *Just Imagine* delighted their audiences by displaying a wide range of technologically advanced consumer goods, especially televisions- a movie staple since at least 1924 – picture phones, and the private aircraft, the ultimate vehicle for individual mobility.

34 Hugh Ferriss Isolated Masses: Towers of Street and Glass.

This perspective layout carried the following comment from the architect: "though the public continues through habit, to conceive structural strength in terms of masonry, they will not continue to misinterpret, for the public's indulgence, the new language of steel; in a building where the load is carried more on the interior than the exterior column, they will not place a façade which states falsely, that the greatest load is carried on the corners".

35 Hugh Ferriss Skyscrapers Spanning Streets

Broad superhighways establish a geometric ground plan that extends upward through overlapping levels of bridges, terraced walkways, and streets. The grid of circulation systems is pierced by enormously high free-standing skyscrapers surrounded by lower setback buildings. Having created this design as an analogy to the natural world of "towering mountain peaks, surrounded by foothills," appreciation of individual towers was impossible when the towers were closely spaced.

36-37 Entrance Civic and Business Center of Meadow City, New Jersey.

This pen and ink drawing depicts an Art Deco inspired design for the entrance to the future civic and business center of the proposed Meadows City, at the head of the Hackensack River in New Jersey.

38-39 Industrial Development Hackensack Meadows, New Jersey.

This pencil drawing shows a glimpse of the industrial section of the proposed Hackensack Meadows development. Railroads, waterways, and highways all converge on the areas set aside for manufacturing.

48-53 Achilles G. Rizzoli

The full scope of this introspective and enigmatic architect's voluminous work can be found in the book *A.G. Rizzoli, Architect of Magnificent Visions*. It has writings by Jo Farb Hernandez, John Beardsley and Roger Cardinal. It was published in 1997 by Harry N. Abrams, Inc. New York.

Bonnie Grossman of the Ames Gallery in Berkeley, California, who supplied all the images for this book, holds the copyright on all of Mr. Rizzoli's work.

54-55 Bernard Maybeck Music Temple, Golden Gate Exposition, San Francisco.

This sketch was an early proposal for the 1939 Golden Gate Exposition in San Francisco, California. It was a theme building set in a lagoon. The commission was presented to William G. Merchant, in whose office Maybeck was working at the time. As Maybeck withdrew from practice during 1932-1938, Merchant established his own office at the same address and hired Maybeck to make preliminary designs and sketches for many of his commissions, of which this was one.

56 Iakov Georgievich Chernikov Compositional Invention of Diverse Volumes with Decorative Coloring.

One of the thousands of drawings and designs of imaginary structures included here in an assemblage that resembles a portion of a city of the future. Chernikov was probably the first architect to write a book entitled *Architectural Fantasies*, which was published in 1933. In this book he not only championed imagination in architecture but expressed its necessity for the creative architect, who should first train the imagination. He reached the conclusion that great thinkers of all times gave great importance to fantasy, as being the forerunner of any kind of progress.

57 THINGS TO COME Still image from the film.

The film was based on he screenplay by H.G. Wells' *The shape of Things To Come*. However, he wanted it to be the exact opposite to Fritz Lang's *Metropolis*. What to us seems to predict hotel lobbies of the 1970's with their soaring atriums was achieved by models of transparent materials. With sets designed by Lazlo Maholy-Nagy, the city of the future was somewhat reminiscent of his Bauhaus background.

58 Frank Lloyd Wright Roger Lacey Hotel.

All the principles Wright used in his high-rise buildings; central-core supports, cantilevered floor slabs, nonsupporting screen walls hung from the slabs – were present in this hotel project. Each successive floor of the nine-story main block, and the tower that rises out of it is larger than the one beneath it.

The entire surface of the building was to consist of diamond-shaped panes of double-thickness frosted glass with glass wool insulation. This would allow a softly diffused light to permeate the interior.

59 Frank Lloyd Wright Huntington Hartford Resort.

On the sunset terrace at Taliesin West is a memorial that Mr. Wright designed and built for Mrs. Wright's daughter, Svetlana, who was killed in an automobile accident. The memorial consists of three plowshares at equal points of an equilateral triangle. They are supported by means of a stone and concrete pylon, which rises through the discs to hold a large Arizona quartz crystal over which a small fountain emerges and feeds water into the discs.

Mr. Wright thought that the forms projecting out of the masonry would make an interesting architectural form. He designed just such a form for this project, to be built in a canyon in Hollywood Hills, California.

60-61 Frank Lloyd Wright Pittsburgh Point Civic Center.

This project would be placed where the Allegheny and Monongahela rivers meet, with bridges stretching out to it from their banks. The main spiral was to contain cinemas, convention rooms, opera and symphony halls, an arena, restaurants, shops and other facilities. The entire development was meant to be a beautiful feature at the juncture of the two rivers, and would replace factories that were destroying the natural setting and polluting the entire city.

62-63 Frank Lloyd Wright Twin Cantilevered Bridges.

The vast size and scope of the first design for the Pittsburgh Point Civic Center proved to be too large for the city's requirements. The second scheme features the two bridges required for the river crossings. The bridges are cantilevered off the point by means of a large concrete counterweight, sail-like in form, while cables in equal degrees of tension along the bridge further stabilizes the structures. The night rendering depicts the shimmering beauty of the bridge lights reflected in the water below.

64-65 Bruce Alonzo Goff, John Garvey House, Number 1. Aerial, ground level, and interior perspectives delineated by Herb Greene.

This structure was designed for a university professor of music and his wife, a performing musician. The primary plan was circular. The interior volume was created by curved aluminum struts springing from the center like a fountain. Wire mesh was to span between the struts and hang down from the outer perimeter to complete the enclosure. A layer of transparent coating would be sprayed over the mesh. A film of water flowing over the outer surface would cool the house in summer, and in winter the water was meant to freeze, providing insulation. The interior rooms, contained in aluminum spheres, were positioned at different levels, and would be connected by a spiral tube. Each sphere would be constructed from prefabricated gas storage tanks, and framed by a radiating pattern of aluminum struts.

66-67 Bruce Alonzo Goff, Joe Price Studio, Number 1. Perspective and interior view, delineated by Jim Parent.

This design was never constructed. A second version was built, and expanded with additions over the years. Joe Price set up the Shin'enKan Foundation, where the studio would become a center of learning for architecture. The structure was the victim of arson and burned to the ground.

68-69 Bruce Alonzo Ignacio Perez House, Number 2, Caracas, Venezuela. Perspective from below.

The Department of Architecture at the Art Institute of Chicago was awarded a grant from the National Historical Publications and Records Commission to fund the complete cataloging of all drawings in the Bruce Goff Archive. The Bruce Goff Archive was donated to the Art Institute by the Shin'enKan Foundation in 1990.

The drawings have been the most frequently consulted collections in the Department of Architecture. Research queries come from architects, scholars, homeowners, and students in the United States and around the world.

70 Joseph Wythe Eagle Nest

The following pages, 71 through 97 represent examples of work produced by students of Bruce Goff at the University of Oklahoma during the 1950's. The projects are examples from a course taught only by Bruce Goff, and reflect his vision of the elements of architectural design related to pure design concepts, such as mass, balance, and reflection. He also had them explore elements relating to music, such as rhythm, counterpoint, theme and development. The work of the following people are exhibited in this section:

Herb Greene, Robert Faust, Ernest, James Gardner, Howard Alan, Arthur Kohara, John Hurtig, James Gresham, and Jack Golden.

98-99 Jack Golden Aviary/Aquarium Top Right: Zoo Bottom Right: Restaurant

Jack Golden has been exploring what might be called "organic high-tech," or more properly, an architectural approach applying the principles of organic architecture to highly technological industrial materials and techniques.

The scheme for the restaurant explores this organic high-tech solution, by utilizing various structural components not usually found in conventional systems. The enclosure would consist of a metal skin stretched over a lightweight metal structure (similar to an aircraft wing). It would be entirely balanced by a radial suspension system in which all loads are transferred via a vertical metal derrick to a single foundation, much like a radio or TV transmission tower.

The structure is located in a gorge, and entered by a suspension bridge from the parking area. Dining areas are situated in suspended "capsules" serviced by a series of ramps from the central core. The overall effect would be an enclosure which opens at the upper levels much like the petals of a giant metallic flower.

100-101 Jack Golden Study in Architectural Form: Smooth Modulation.

This drawing was executed as part of the "Elements of Architecture", as taught by architect Bruce Goff at the University of Oklahoma.

102 Howard Alan Top Left: Study in Architectural Form: Counterpoint. Bottom Left: Study in Architectural Form: Irregular Rhythm

This drawing was executed as part of the "Elements of Architecture", as taught by architect Bruce Goff at the University of Oklahoma. The "elements" included references and examples of music terminology.

103 Howard Alan Atomic Power Plant.

This project, which features monumental forms reminiscent of Eric Mendelsohn, was winner of the Clay Products Award from the Texas Society of Architects, Clay Products Association of the Southwest.

106-107 Frank Lloyd Wright Arizona State Capital.

Wright's design for this project was not the result of a direct commission. Rather, it was his statement about what he felt Arizona should build to house its government. He suggested that the project be moved outside of urban Phoenix and into a beautiful park at the city's edge.

Over the entire structure was a great lattice dome of cast concrete and copper, acting as a "shade tree" for the courts below. From this feature the project took its name, "Oasis," and on the perspective was also added the title "Pro Bono Publico Arizona."

108-109 Frank Lloyd Wright Living City Project.

This view of the landscape developed from the Broadacre City project, designed between the 1930's to the 1950's, included an example of practically every building type that Mr. Wright designed in his whole career.

110-111 Bruce Alonzo Goff Left: First National Bank, Independence, MO: Perspective, delineated by Larry W. Grantham.

113-115 Archigram: Peter Cook Plug-In City: Longitudinal Section. Below: University Node.

At a casual glance *Plug-in City* appears to be a common megastructure, as there are the familiar diagonals of the load-bearing frame and the prefabricated infill cells. In fact, nothing could be farther from the intent than to present a blueprint for another orderly and tedious mega-city.

Plug-in City is an open-ended structure. It has no definitive form. Instead it has a plan reminiscent of the layout of a medieval town. As little as possible is predetermined, in order to allow the greatest possible scope for growth and regeneration. The entire city is intended to replace itself, with the aid of its omnipresent cranes, every 40 years. There is meant to be a constant activity of swapping new components for old, as new technologies and needs make existing facilities obsolete.

A city which can extend, exchange, remove itself without affecting its ultimate stability is the paramount goal. The exuberant variety of building form's in the City, the loving attention given to tiny units dangling at the end of cranes waiting to be popped into the nearest available hole, the hovering office buildings in the river – all are calculated to escape from architectural dreariness.

The futuristic trappings are all part of the message. Architecture is not permanent; the passwords are expendability, indeterminacy, exchange, and removal. *Plug-in City* is an intermediate step toward true adaptability in which the environment will be limited only by the individual's imagination.

116-117 Archigram: Ron Herron *Walking Cities*

Cities: Moving; Master Vehicle-Habitation 1964 elevation

The "master vehicle" shown here in elevation is only one of several units of the *Walking City*. It is by far the most frequently reproduced Archigram image. The City is composed of an indefinite number of such units, each containing different urban areas and residential districts, and all linked by retractable corridors. These containers with controlled micro-climates have retractable sun-roofs, roam the landscape, grouping and re-grouping at will,

The *Walking City* is an expression in architectural terms of the Archigram vision of society. The social structure of cities is not static; mobility, flexibility, and change are the dominant characteristics of modern urban life.

Walking Cities Above: Invading New York.
Below: *Walking Cities* In the Desert.

118-119 Paolo Soleri

Top Left: Novanoah I. Bottom Left: Novanoah II. (119) Detail of Novanoah II. Paolo Soleri's radical concepts graphically reflects his revolutionary philosophy in which humankind progresses from a chaotic level on which solutions are fragmentary, through a more sophisticated stage of patterned thought (urban sprawl), to a level where architecture is synthesized with ecology and cities are conceived as single buildings. This is his view of miniaturization.

Soleri is best known for his arcologies, the word he coined as a fusion of two words: architecture and ecology. One of his arcologies, Arconsanti is an experimental project under construction for 3,000 people using only 10 acres within an 860 acre land sanctuary. When completed, the town will rise 15 stories, and will serve as a study center for the social, economic, and ecological implications of its architectural framework.

120 Paolo Soleri

Top and Bottom Left: 3-D Jersey.

3-D Jersey was designed as an urban transportation nucleus in the state of New Jersey, located in the New York - Philadelphia corridor. The main structure of the transportation center covers about one square mile and is about ½ mile high. The city is circular in plan, and designed to house a million people. Industrial and warehouse spaces radiate from the main structure and would be covered with parks and gardens.

The entire site including park area covers less than 14 square miles. It was designed to solve the problem of connecting air travel with a new urban center in a direct manner, integrating the air facilities into the matrix of the system, instead of as an appendage. This new arcology incorporates a circular jet runway ringing the entire 14-square-mile site with long underground air-taxi corridors leading towards the central city structure. (Isometric Drawing by Junji Shirai).

121 Paolo Soleri Hexahedron.

122-123 Herb Greene Exhibition Hall / Civic Arena.

This pen and ink drawing represents methods of renovating urban areas by creating "armatures" of new structures attached to existing ones. Overlapping time frames are suggested by the inclusion of historic buildings. The encrusted base is reminiscent of archaeological layers balanced against the high technology roof structure.

In designing loose fitting frameworks for armatures architects may provide a collage of cues; a heavy, rough, earthy component and, in contrast, the smoothness, transparency and weightlessness that can b e obtained by new technologies.

The courtyard under the roof membrane can be cooled by re-circulated water flowing over its exterior surface. Qualities of old and new, massiveness and lightness, warmth and coolness, afforded by these contrasts are capable of harmonizing most additions.

122 Eugene Ray Bottom Left: Everett Solar Heated Villa, Lyons Valley, California.

This two-story solar heated residence has four greenhouses on the south side, and double towers with rooms for sleeping under the stars during the summer months.

123 Eugene Ray Bottom Right: Freeman Solar Heated Villa, Morro Bay, California.

This project was a garden-oriented, multi-level, prototype residence with an outdoor swimming pool.

125 Jacques Gillet Sketches of a Tomb for "My Friend Bruce Goff" (Colored pencil, 1983)

These three images are part of a series of eleven sketches that architect Jacques Gillet drew to describe his feelings on the death of architect Bruce Goff. They were inspired in part by the "Eleven Famous Bridges of Diverse Provinces" by the Japanese artist Hokusai.

128 Syd Mead Top: Golf Course Clubhouse.

This project was designed for a proposed golf course project in Chiba Prefecture, Japan. The "Green" design was a solution for environmental preservation constraints.

Bottom: Tokyo Night Club; Space Club

This drawing was an idea for a theme entertainmen complex with peripheral observation track offering an overall view before an actual visit to various attractions at the club.

129 Syd Mead Top: Minolta Marina.

This illustration was created for Minolta Camera as a romantic, fantastic view of a scene that would be a "photo op" for anyone with a Minolta camera.

Bottom: Affrox: Linear City.

This illustration was created as part of a corporate campaign, this linear city is actually an enormous hexagonal beam, stretching from the bay floor to a coastal mountaintop.

130-131 Stanley Tigerman Top: New York City. Bottom: Lakeside. (131) Top: Career Collage. Bottom: Myrtle Beach.

Visionary architect Stanley Tigerman was also a prolific sketch artist, depicting his architectural concepts. He describes them as follows: "my drawings are both front and back, retrograde and optimistic. They are fantasy based, yet pragmatic and realty based, because they are architecture".

132-Eugene Tsui Top left: Torrevista, Studio of Eugene Tsui, Tejiras, New Mexico.

Seven levels of circular floors provide a 360 degree sweeping panorama of desert and mountains. The use of a hyperboloid presents an economical solution to a multi-level. Multi-purpose residence where unobstructed views are desired. The structure is constructed of straight wood planks paired and bolted at the points of intersection. Repeating panels of imprinted fiberglass and rigid insulation are placed in the diamond-shaped openings.

Bottom left: Solarrius; Passive Solar Energy Center for the Arctic Pipeline Company.

This research facility was designed in response to the client's interest in understanding the effectiveness of various building forms in a very cold climate. The low angle design is intended to maximize solar heat efficiency by directing sunlight to the interior spaces and recirculating warm air currents throughout.

133 Eugene Tsui Above: House on a Cliff, San Francisco.

This house is a "visitation" prototype open for public viewing. The structure appears to soar outward. The underside is curved and perforated to dispel strong updrafts. A collapsible. convertible lookout "pod" offers a sweeping view of the San Francisco Bay.

Below: Prototype Ravine Windmill Dwelling, Orinda, California.

This design includes a residence and optometry office accessible to clients from the bottom of a ravine. Structurally, the house is a catanary arch bridge supported by a central stairway core. The triangulated structural plan provides stable and strong anchoring into the earth at three points.

Aerodynamic in design, a windmill is also integral with this house. A passive solar "crown" adjusts to the changing angles of the sun.

134 Eugene Tsui Office/Apartment/Research Tower for the Apple Computer Corporation.

This design eliminates the problem of daily vehicular commuting from home to work. It proposes large condominiums with office and research facilities in one integral structure, with underground parking and a small-scale shopping mall. The building is partially powered by photovoltaic solar cells and a passive solar water tank. Research, manufacturing and office facilities are located at the lower levels with residential condominiums at the upper floors.

136 Davis Bite` Study in Mass for a Cathedral.

This crisp pen-and-ink line drawing emphasizes the angularity and expressiveness of the monumental forms, which are echoes in the up-turned corners of the religious habit's headdress. The treatment of the site and rendition of landscaping heighten the dramatic effect.

141 Douglas Cooper The Approach.

This intricately detailed drawing exemplifies the artists "split projection" technique. It represents two or more points of view in a single drawing. As a whole it is a collage of views rather than a singular view. In this case the left side of the image illustrates a perspective view from below the objects receding back into space. The right side illustrates the same structures from slightly above, yet they look like a composite whole.

142-143 Hans Christian Lischewski Media House for Karl Friedrich Schinkel.

This project was an entry in a design competition, and not only used computer graphics as a visualization tool, but conceptualized various applications of this technology into the design itself.

Schinkel generated numerous alternatives for a specified design project. He also was involved in stage set design for the Berlin Opera House. Taking these two concepts as a base, and projecting them into the twentieth century, placed him in Los Angeles, close to the film industry, and near the computer industry of Silicon Valley in northern California.

The house façade is a large screen, which in the daytime plots large ink-jet images over the whole area. At night, video and computer graphics are projected onto the screen. The images are constantly changing, displaying design exercises or avante-garde computer graphics displays.

The complex is equipped with high-tech sensors, directed towards the street to detect movement, and transfer them through a computer program into visual displays on the façade during the night hours.

144 Orest Places for People in 2010: Terrestrial.

This project is a 210 story megastructure on the outskirts of Los Angeles. It contains offices, residential, hotel, retail, educational and recreational facilities. It featured a rapid transit station, a people-mover and a monorail system. It is in the middle of a 100 acre man-made lake with marinas and water related facilities

145 Orest Places for People in 2010: Extraterrestrial.

This is the extraterrestrial version of the space station city, orbiting the planet earth. The structure is 420 stories high, with a proposed population of 30,000 inhabitants. It contained shuttle docking facilities, and other advanced forms of space travel systems.

146 Harvey Ferraro Test Tubes-R-Us.

As an alternative to fashionable architectural thinking, this work concerns the modulation of light, form, and the visual properties of materials. Parallel to the process of growth in nature, organic elements conceived in a state of change are characterized by the role of light in a visual dialogue. The vertical transformation is shown by an opaque cluster of organic forms at the base, rising through translucent forms to transparent crystalline forms at the apex.

148-149 Harvey Ferraro / Gretchen Marick Movie Set Design.

This combined work applies organic and mechanistic forms to a monumental set design for a movie.

150-151 Richard Rogers Partnership Tokyo International Forum. Design Competition.

This competition entry was a multi-purpose cultural and convention center on the site of the old city hall in Tokyo. This striking design had an exposed structural frame supporting three auditoria expressed as steel-plated capsules suspended from the top of the frame.

152-153 Martin Meyers Mural with an Architectural Theme.

Architects Bregman and Hamann in Toronto, Canada commissioned this mural for an 8 foot by 30 foot wall. The wall had a column in the middle, so the mural was divided in half; one side representing ancient architecture and the other side modern themes.

The drawings were done on individual panels by projecting the design sketches onto the panels, drawing first in pencil, then with ink; and finally adding details in watercolor.

155 Gordon Grice Fixing Our Future.

This dystopian image was commissioned for the cover of a Toronto business directory. The city of Toronto is identified by the CN Tower among the other buildings. The city is shown in an ordered-disorderly fashion, as if in a distant chaotic future.

156 Lee Dunnette Astronaut's Memorial.

This pastel drawing depicts a hypothetical ruin of the 20th Century, on the shores of an unknown ocean.

157 Arthur Cotton Moore Top: Decorative Rooftop Exhaust Fans. Bottom: Asymmetrical Pipe Capital with Industrial Light Fixture.

There is a tradition among architects to extend their work into more artistic realms, moving from the blueprint to the paintbrush. Arthur Cotton Moore has turned to ink, watercolor washes and acrylic to portray a new development in his own style, Industrial Baroque. The paintings often begin as a drawing. They are made into a slide and projected onto a large canvas for the basic outline.

Although the drawings refer to techniques and coloration of the Renaissance, it is on the dynamism and theatricality of Italian Baroque architecture that he draws a transformation of the rectilinear aspects of modernist architecture. Moore's art in technique and in content is an architecture of unifying contrasts, exploring the nuances of color and texture, and elaborating a pictorial drama of line and plane. Through this synthetic vision the language of the Renaissance works together with the modern, producing a unique architecture.

158 Lebbeus Woods City of Air.

Lebbeus Woods is like a contemporary Piranesi, who returns to pre-modern history to redefine the future; based on science, dominated by technology, and holistically including philosophy, architecture, art, and the entire range of engineering and natural sciences.

His graphic universe is both enigmatic and familiar. It abounds with forms that recall domes, balloon-like cupolas, or airships like flying Noah's arcs, extra-terrestrial architectural bodies that defy the familiar laws of geometry and gravity.

159-161 Lebbeus Woods (159) Aerial Paris. (161) Above: War and Architecture. Below: War and Architecture.

"Invention and transformation are the aspects of architectural form that I explore in my drawings. These aspects best represent the spirit of our restless culture and suggest that only a dynamic architecture can express its underlying methods and goals. It is significant that nature itself evolves by similar means, indicating that architecture is meant to reflect the complex cyclic patterns and rhythms of nature.

The interplay of architecture, culture, and nature is dramatically affected by light, the subject of our most profound perceptions. The fantastic regions I describe in my drawings explore the presence of light, revealing its role in the creation of dynamic forms and their mutation through continuous experimentation. Color is a primary property of light and thus indispensable in my research".

165 James Rossant Above: Cities in the Sky #3, Below: #4.

The drawings have varied districts and neighborhoods, and full blown city centers. The center of City #4 is a complex place with a new kind of downtown. Here is a busy city center with enormous administration and business buildings. There are city squares in space, and beyond are suburban neighborhoods of loft buildings set in gardens. Floating nearby are special function structures, such as the high amphitheater complex in the upper right of the drawing.

166-167 James Rossant Cities in the Sky.

This drawing explores the set of linear communities in the sky. Clusters arise fed by the parallel streets, but without a consistent series of crossings from one community corridor to the other, as in a city based on a grid. Clusters of forms that are built on these parallel streets merge and make cross communications possible. There are endless possibilities of linkages, but they must be discovered or invented. The city has some of the properties of a rational grid, but also the depth of interest of an organic city.

169-171 Ian McKay Babel- The Infinite City: #1. #2, #3.

A series of works produced for exhibition and publication, with the theme "The Tower of Babel and Other Follies," this piece was built up as an improvisation on an axonometric grid. The Tower of Babel, in reaching for an infinite heaven, must be infinite in scale. Having no horizon, the axonometric drawing may theoretically reach to infinity.

172 Frank M. Costantino Hancock Axial I.

A self-commissioned work expressing the concept of a second skyscraper structure, paralleling the major axis of one of Boston's boulevards, to penetrate the monolithic form of I.M. Pei's Hancock Tower. The building's color, scale and orientation would complement the existing one, and indicates the artist's interest in layered watercolor washes and the fascination with steam.

173 Jeffrey Michael George New De Anza Hotel.

Created in another era less restrictive of the imagination, this architectural fantasy explores the future possibilities of an existing urban hotel. The establishment not only accommodates but encourages the fantasies of its guests. The design of the structure was inspired, both formally and spiritually, by the ancient Egyptian civilization.

176-179 Nancy Wolf

Twentieth Century visionary architecture is about new technologies and new materials, new processes and computers. It is about tearing down and building up. It is about change. But this is a technological vision – a vision that either forgets or denies its human inhabitants. Architects are able to create the perfectionism and cool precision of modernism; the opulence and commodification of postmodernism; the ideological disturbances of deconstructivism; and the retro-style of the new urbanism.

Where do people fit into these architectural post-human landscapes? My art is about a vision of people lost and disconnected from such high-tech dreams and realities. It portrays people as they disappear - confused, overwhelmed, and alone – into these new spaces of their own and others' making.

In my work over the past twenty-five years, I have protested against these cement, glass, and metallic landscapes. When I leave my studio and walk through these desolate landscapes I become one of the figures I am portraying. These years have been intense and lonely, punctuated by the delight of encountering and imaging the figures I portray in my art.

As Aldo van Eyck so poignantly wrote in the 1950's about humankind's "pre-urban" longing for a sense of place in these restless new visionary vistas. "Space has no room, not for a moment for man, he is excluded. In order to help him - help his homecoming – he must be gathered into their meaning (man is the subject as well as the object of architecture).

Whatever space and time mean, place and occasion mean more. For space in the image of man is place, and time in the image of man is occasion. Today, space and what it should coincide within order to become "space" – man at home with himself – are lost. Both search for the same place, but cannot find it. Provide that place.

180 Tad Berezowski Imaginary Tower Designs.

More than any other form of architectural expression, the tower is distinctly American in character. It is a structural form born of economic prudence, as American real estate developers have traditionally sought to build as much rentable space as possible on sites located in overcrowded urban settings. Aesthetically, modern tower design is primarily an exercise in composing the architectonic elements on a building's facades so as to prevent monstrous, stark surfaces from dominating the structure's skin.

Adopting a gothic structural image, this tower's facades are dominated by three upwardly thrusting vertical elements. The central, superior segment is capped with a solar and radio collector dish, symbolizing the importance of new space technology in everyday life and commerce.

The intent in this design was to echo the proportions of the human body, which has been classically determined to be ten heads high. Composed of three main elements, a base (feet), an intermediate section (body), and top (neck and head), this tower has an extended neck to allow the head (a replica of the solar system with the earth located at its upper extremity) to be seen from the ground

181 Tad Berezowski Imaginary Villa.

Traditionally, a villa has been a place to retire from the turmoil of the city and enjoy gardens, fountains, and the peace inherent in country life. A villa has no prescribed form, since guidelines for designing a leisure environment lack clear definition. As a result, villa design has historically been one of the most innovative types of architecture. This design emphasizes no active interaction between the villa and its surroundings. Sitting on a water platform, the villa becomes a sculptural object.

Ceremonial entry to the salon and garden occurs on the ground level. The second level accommodates all daily household functions, and the third is a private quarter with access to a roof deck. An introverted scheme, this villa offers its inhabitants total isolation from the outside world. On the ground floor, no windows open to the surrounding countryside. Only from the atelier on the second floor can visual contact be made with the outlying environment. A large, outdoor courtyard provides the house with a ceremonial space for diverse uses such as theatrical presentations, musical concerts, exhibitions, and public receptions.

182 Paul Laffoly GEOCHRONMECHANE: The Time Machine From Earth.

1995 marked the 100th anniversary of the publication of the famous novel by H.G. Wells – *The Time Machine.* Will there be a practical working model of a time machine ready for common use? Paul Laffoly's homage to H.G.Wells, Buckminister Fuller, and others, is a visual compilation of those ideas on canvas.

183 Paul Laffoly Quartum Dimensio Aedificium.

The design of this municipal building was intended to act as an economic catalyst, which in turn would provide the impetus and the necessary tax base for the emergent Massachusetts City of Mandela – to be named in honor of Nelson Mandela of South Africa.

The goal of the structure is to focus the energies of the existing people of emerging Mandela in much the same way that the building of Medieval cathedrals did. That is, the town's entire population would be involved, making the cathedral their own.

The multi-use structure would be built using traditional African imagery, and besides reinforced concrete and steel would use natural woods, grasses, trees, grafted vegetation, animal bones and the like.

183 Paul Laffoly Das Urpflanze Haus.

The site for this house is to be located on a freshwater lake or island, with specific biological properties to support vegetation. The structure is made up of three distinct varieties of trees, layered from the base upward. The entire house is based on a biological architectural mode.

The only form of life that will ultimately survive in the universe is the primordial plant (urpflanze). It does not need the earth or any earthly environment to survive. It is plants that have made the earth a survivable environment for all other species of life. "Das Urpflanze Haus is but a flower of the world tree house. I call it the earth flower." Paul Laffoly

184-185 Manuel Avila City in the Future.

A futuristic theme dominates this pen-and-ink drawing showing a vision of the future from inside an air ship, complete with a robo-pilot.

186-187 Ernest Burden III Organic bridge.

This pencil drawing explores the characteristics of an organic bridge structure, based on natural forms, becoming a bridge habitat spanning a body of water.

188-189 Kevin Woest Bridge Habitat: Detail of tower and overall view.

When a simple bridge structure is augmented by space that can be occupied, it forms a bridge habitat. The revenues from these spaces can be dedicated to the financing and ongoing maintenance of the structure.

This example integrates residential and office functions within a bridge for New York City where land values are extremely high. Other recommended functions for a bridge's habitat include: schools, healthcare facilities, justice and penal facilities, commercial and recreation.

Bridges span water or dramatic topographies which are aesthetically pleasing, even inspirational. Accordingly, bridge sites offer highly desirable environments for working, learning, living and playing.

190 Richard Ferrier Above: Windows and Fragments: Memory and Desire.

This highly organized and subtle drawing and construction provides an abstract method of exploring the juxtaposition of architectural and artistic elements.

Below: Detail from Ousley Watercolor.

An abstract drawing done for a client prior to the development of the actual design.

192 Robert McIlhargey Left: Space Park, Breman, Germany. New World Entertainment Complex, Hawaii. Owners: OMNI Corporation, Los Angeles, CA. Waisman Dewar Grant Carter Architects.

194 Christopher Grubbs Entrance to Ikpiari, Tokyo, Japan. Architect: Paul Ma Design, Emeryville, CA.

The most important idea in the design of this unique center for entertainment, commerce and learning was to celebrate change in life, specifically the passage of time. At the entrance, at the stroke of midnight, the great dial would shift to the symbol of the new day represented by icons from different world cultures.

195 David Joiner Galaxeum: Proposed Space Museum, Observatory and Planetarium.

This conceptual project was designed for the residual use of the 1982 World's Fair in Knoxville, Tennessee. It would contain an auditorium, classroom and workshop facilities, and a gift shop.

196 Sergei Tchoban Monument.

The unique perspective juxtaposition of the two images which overlap in one drawing is characteristic of this artist/designer's work. The forced perspective dramatizes the height of the monument, while the radiating lines from the site design become rays of light in the sky of the adjacent ground level viewpoint.

198-199 James Akers Battersea Power Station Development Project, London.

This preliminary sketch for a restaurant environment has all the qualities of a Piranesi sketch, both in treatment and architectural detail.

200-201 Thomas W. Schaller Orpheus in Orlando.

This watercolor painting represents a modernists retelling of the classic myth of Orpheus; where our hero finds that the underworld has become the province of a large-scale corporate development firm.

203 James Parakh Opposite: Office Towers above Penn Station.

As an experiment and exploration of new media and ideas, this theoretical drawing explores the notion of a multi-programmed "vertical street," allowing various functions (health clubs, library, disco) to mix with conventional office space.

207 Yves Rathle Left: Bagna mixed-use tower, Bankok, Thailand.

This structure combines a 57 story corporate headquarters, a 5-story convention center, and a 35-story condominium in a mixed-use project for Bangkok, Thailand. The client was design 103, Ltd.

207 Yves Rathle Above and Below: HMV/Rock and Roll Hall of Fame , Prototype Theme Store.

This project was a study in mixing an entertainment museum with a retail environment, and turning it into a public attraction. The client was Elkus/Manfredi and HMV Records.

208 Imre Makovecz Above: Sketch of Tower: Lutheran Church, Siofok.

This sketch was the first design for the church tower. But the project went unrealized. It was finally built with a much simpler form, which included the face of an unidentified being who had wings located above the eyes.

Wings, angels and towers are often connected in Mackovecz's designs.

208 Imre Makovecz Below: Sketch, Church of Kolozsvar (Cluj – Romania).

The sketches for this design, which echoes early local timber structures, shows angels running in the streets, a symbol of the frustration within the cultural context and the overall planning process.

209 Imre Makovecz The Bartok Performances: Stage Set Construction.

The constructions were built for three different performances of the work of composer Bela Bartok. They were moved into different positions for each performance to match the character of the music.

210 Sadaka Kinuta Concerto.

This imaginary building personifies the image of music; as if the performances inside flowed outside to the building itself, the earth and the sky.

210 Stephan Hoffpauir Sony Station: Virtual Theme Park.

The drawing was intended to be the first page of an internet web site. It portrays an imaginary theme park whose concept and buildings were based on Sony products. Visitors to the site were to click on individual areas of the drawing, and would then be taken to close-up drawings of these locations. The park sits on an imaginary island. The giant floating CDs gives the viewer a clue that the place exists in a world outside of real time and space. The "Moderne" architectural motifs, inspired by the 1939 New York World's Fair, are used to suggest an exciting yet non-threatening future based on technology.

211 Hans Christian Lischewski Cybercities.

The project was developed by the Mediatecture Group in 1997. The client, Direct Interactive, Inc., wanted to create a number of cybercities as virtual environments for internet-based commerce and entertainment. Six different cities would float in space and form colonies of satellites. Each would have their own source of energy, and all were accessible through a docking station at the bottom of the structure.

Paying subscribers of this service would run their real-time travel sequences from a CD-ROM that would contain all the necessary segments and their links. The subscriber would be logged-on to a live Website that would provide the person with real-time, instant access to various databases of banking, shopping and other activities.

The form and appearance of each structure reflects the function they contain. It is "architecture for the cybermasses. Circulation is provided for "physically exhausted" visitors to travel between buildings in individual cars, guided by an electronic rail system.

212-213 Batman Forever Concept sketches for scenery and backgrounds for the Warner Bros. Film.

Fifty years after Batman's debut as a comic strip in 1939, a movie studio turned the theme into a major motion picture. It created a gloomy, nightmarish city that was neither historically nor geographically identifiable, but one that remained convincing as a somewhat familiar metropolis.

A large number of conceptual sketches were produced to be later translated into models, large-scale sets, and matte paintings. The drawings and interviews reveal how the city was designed around a number of carefully chosen parameters. The city was neither futuristic nor historical. It was to be as timeless as possible.

Since they were drawing from the original comic strip for inspiration - there was bound to be a certain '40s feeling to it. They maximized space, bridged over streets, and built the buildings cantilevering out over the streets rather than away from them.

The director translated images of architecture, not architecture itself, into set designs. He created an array of unadorned, structurally expressive, industrialized buildings, a dark resume of a century of architectural modernism. In striking contrast, Batman himself lived in a historic country house.

214 THE FIFTH ELEMENT Above: Still image from Columbia Picture's science fiction fantasy
(Computer image by: Digital Domain#11 1998)   Set in New York in in the 23rd century this film is a composite of mixed media – namely miniature models and Computer graphics imagery and animation.

214 STAR WARS, Episode One: The Phantom Menace. Still image from the film.

This scene from the epic movie shows a conference taking place between many of the main characters. Beyond the room, one can get a glimpse of the environment of the planet they were on – which was totally covered with cities.

215 BLADERUNNER Above: Still image, street scene from the film.

The premise in this film is not only the connection to *Metropolis*, to which *BladeRunner* owes much in terms of ideas for individual settings and imagery of the city. The architectural treatment of the main character's apartment was inspired by and partially filmed at Frank Lloyd Wright's Ennis House in Los Angeles.

A key concept for the design of the city's architecture was that of "retrofitting" or "layering" – the continuous repair and adaptation to changing needs, which led to the imagery of buildings covered by webs of pipes, ducts, and technological debris. Visions of monolithic cities for hundreds of people were believed to contain the essential ideas for future town planning.

215 THE FIFTH ELEMENT Above: Still image from Columbia Picture's science fiction fantasy
(Computer image by: Digital Domain#11 1998).

216-217 Ernest Burden III Exile: From a Prison's Portfolio, after Piranesi's Il Carceri.

218-219 WHAT DREAMS MAY COME Still image from the film (1999).

Using high-end computer software the animators for this film created one sequence of 20 shots of matte paintings showing an elaborate city, with architecture from many different periods, nesting in the clouds across from a vast abyss. Everything is animated, from the streams crashing over the waterfalls to the shadows of clouds as they move over the city.

A live-action element puts Robin Williams and dozens of extras on a staircase – filmed against a green screen – and then composited together for this scene.

Index